THE Saltwater Cookbook

FISH AND SEAFOOD FROM OCEAN TO TABLE

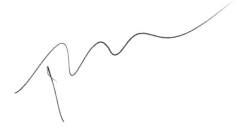

TIM LAUER

CREATIVE PUBLISHING international

CHANHASSEN, MINNESOTA

www.creativepub.com

TIM LAUER has taught cooking classes at such prestigious locations as Coastal Seafoods Cooking School, Cooks of Crocus Hill, and American Heart Institute. Tim has served as Executive Chef for Quail Catering & Restaurant and Nigel's Restaurant, as well as Sous Chef for the Minneapolis Athletic Club. He lives in Minnesota, where he is General Manager at Coastal Seafoods.

ACKNOWLEDGMENTS

I would like to thank the many dedicated seafood professionals with whom I have worked over the past thirty years. Without their generous sharing of knowledge I never would have enjoyed my career as much as I have.

The most special thanks goes to my family who was my biggest inspiration and was supportive beyond belief.

Finally, I am grateful for my son Sam's computer skills, which quite literally allowed this book to be written.

Copyright © 2004 by Creative Publishing international, Inc.
18705 Lake Drive East
Chanhassen, MN 55317
1-800-328-3895
www.creativepub.com

President/CEO: Michael Eleftheriou
Vice President/Publisher: Linda Ball
Vice President/Retail Sales & Marketing: Kevin Haas
Executive Editor, Outdoor Group: Barbara Harold
Creative Director: Brad Springer
Editor: Teresa Marrone
Project Manager: Tracy Stanley
Photo Editor: Angela Hartwell
Studio Services Manager: Jeanette Moss McCurdy
Photographer: Tate Carlson
Assistant Photographer: Herb Schnabel
Food and Prop Stylist: Abigail Wyckoff
Assistant Food Stylists: Susan Telleen, Pegi Lee
Director, Production Services: Kim Gerber
Production Manager: Helga Thielen

Printed on American paper by: R. R. Donnelley
10 9 8 7 6 5 4 3 2 1

THE SALTWATER COOKBOOK
by Tim Lauer

Contributing Photographers:
  Dean Abramson, Mainephoto.com,© Dean Abramson: p. 9.
  William Boyce, Boyceimage.com, © William Boyce: p. 12.
  Paul M. Franklin, Pmfranklin.com, © Paul M. Franklin: p. 32.
  John B. Hyde, Wildthingsphotography.com,
    © John B. Hyde: p. 11.
  Evelyn Letfuss, New York, NY, © Evelyn Letfuss: p. 16.
  Brian Parker/Tom Stack & Associates, Key Largo, FL,
    © Brian Parker: p. 6.

Contributing Illustrator: Tom Wallerick

Library of Congress Cataloging-in-Publication Data
Lauer, Tim.
   The saltwater cookbook : fish and seafood : from ocean to table / by Tim Lauer.
     p. cm.
   Includes index.
   ISBN 1-58923-128-7
   1. Cookery (Seafood)   I. Title.
   TX747.L33 2003
   658.3--dc22
                                          2003055442

THE SALTWATER COOKBOOK

CONTENTS

Our oceans provide us with an incredible variety of exciting and unique seafood. Well over 100,000 edible species exist — some well known and commonly used for hundreds of years, others barely seen outside of isolated geographical pockets. In my job as general manager of Coastal Seafoods, a major fish market in the Minneapolis–St. Paul area, every day I see beautiful, pristine opah, ono and fresh tuna, species which until recently were only available in very limited quantities in local markets.

No other protein source provides the cook as many choices as does seafood. With this myriad of options comes the seemingly daunting task of preparation. How do we find appropriate cooking methods and recipes for such a wide-ranging food?

The very characteristics that make seafood such a wonderful and rewarding food can be confusing and intimidating to many cooks. As a result, although worldwide consumption of seafood continues to increase, over seventy percent of all seafood is now consumed in restaurants, where consumers often feel more at ease and confident in the preparations.

This cookbook is designed to take the worry out of seafood cookery by breaking preparation into simple, easily duplicated steps. In the twenty years I've taught over ten thousand people to cook a wide array of seafood, I've been consistently amazed by how easily students with virtually no cooking experience can prepare great tasting, beautiful and healthy seafood with simple, basic guidance. Whether you buy your seafood at a supermarket or fish store, or catch your own, this book can help you have a rewarding and successful seafood experience.

Tim Lauer

CHAPTER ONE

Purchasing Seafood

According to the National Fisheries Institute, over seventy percent of the seafood consumed in America is eaten at restaurants; at-home preparation accounts for just two percent of the seafood in the average American diet. When you ask a group of Americans why they don't cook seafood more often at home, two answers are commonly given. Most people don't know how, when or where to purchase seafood; and once they have purchased (or caught) it, they don't know what to do with it. Most of us grew up eating meat as our main protein source, and have never really become comfortable with the basic rules for handling and cooking seafood.

Where to Buy

The first question that comes up when purchasing seafood is, where should we go? Most grocery stores now sell both fresh and frozen seafood. Many metropolitan areas boast smaller, more specialized seafood markets. Finally, a growing source for seafood purchases are the relatively new supercenter stores that sell everything from tires to salmon in a warehouse-type setting, often at very competitive pricing.

For most of us, convenience will dictate where and when we purchase seafood; however, each source has its own advantages. Buying at a grocery store or supermarket is often the most convenient. Here we can purchase everything we need for the meal at the same time. Additionally, most supermarkets now have a fairly wide array of fresh and frozen seafood. The support or advice we get here can vary considerably. Specialty seafood markets usually sell the largest variety of seafood, and often provide a personal touch with lots of advice and support for less experienced consumers. Finally, the new super-

centers offer the conveniences of a vast range of product and usually have very attractive prices on their somewhat limited seafood choices. The support we receive on seafood purchases at these stores is quite limited.

Fresh or Frozen

The next question to ponder is, should we buy fresh or frozen? Fresh seafood is simply seafood that has never been frozen. Given a choice of perfect fresh or perfect frozen seafood, I prefer fresh; however, the choice is not always so simple. Top-quality frozen fish may be a better choice than marginal or over-the-hill "fresh" fish. When you're buying fish and seafood, always stress quality first. Over the years, frozen seafood has acquired a questionable reputation. Too often, poor-quality "fresh" seafood is frozen, resulting in even lower-quality frozen seafood. Freezing did not create the poor-quality product; the marginal seafood is at the root of the problem.

For top-quality meals, it is essential to start with top-quality seafood. There is simply no way to make poor-quality seafood taste good, and it is simple to make prime seafood taste great. Top-quality seafood, whether fresh or frozen, shows some very clear, consistent signs:

• It should look bright, shiny and attractive.

• There should be no strong or unpleasant ammoniated odors.

• The flesh should be firm and resilient.

• Gills, bloodlines and other "blood" areas should be bright red or pink, rather than gray or brown.

Fin Fish or Shellfish

The next question is what form to purchase seafood in. "Seafood," as it is used here, includes two distinct categories: fin fish and shellfish (including mollusks). Each category has its own considerations.

Let's start with fin fish, which includes species ranging from tiny sardines, to moderately sized salmon, to giant halibut. Following is a brief description of the basic forms fin fish may come in.

Round or whole: This is how fish come from the water, with everything still intact.

Dressed: This is whole fish that have had the entrails removed (gutted). To preserve quality, dressing should take place as soon as possible after the fish has been killed.

Dressed and scaled: Sometimes referred to as "D and S," this refers to whole fish that have been gutted and scaled.

Pan ready: Dressed and scaled fish that have the head, gills, fins and tails removed.

Fillets: Horizontal or lengthwise sides cut from the backbone of a fish.

Steaks: Vertical or crosswise cuts (usually from larger fish) with the bones left in.

It's generally easier and more economical to purchase fish in the form you plan to use. If your recipe calls for fillets, buy fillets; if steaks are called for, buy steaks.

Shellfish typically come in one of four forms: live, shucked, cooked or frozen. The form you buy will depend not only on your recipe but also on the species of shellfish you are buying. Following are brief descriptions of the commonly available shellfish forms.

Live: Lobsters, clams, mussels, oysters, crayfish and crabs are commonly sold live. Lobsters, crabs and crayfish should be heavy for their size and show obvious signs of movement. Mussels, clams and oysters can be open or closed but if open they should respond to light tapping by closing their shells.

Shucked: Oysters, scallops, clams and mussels are all available as shucked products. These shellfish should be firm and have a "fresh" briny smell to them. Strong sulfurous or ammoniated smells should be taken as a dire warning of poor quality.

Cooked: Crabs, crab legs, crab meat and lobster meat are often sold cooked, either fresh or frozen. These are all ready to eat and can be reheated or served as is.

Frozen: Shrimp and lobster tails are most commonly sold as a frozen but uncooked product. Freezing is the best way to preserve these extremely perishable shellfish. For convenience, grocery stores often thaw previously frozen shellfish before sale.

Buying or catching shellfish is quite different from

buying or catching fin fish. Molluscan shellfish, in particular, have some unique properties. Oysters, mussels and clams are filter feeders and therefore can accumulate impurities from the waters they inhabit. Some simple guidelines include:

• Buy molluscan shellfish only from reputable, licensed dealers.

• Make sure dealers have legally required certification tags on file, which do much to guarantee water safety and purity for each harvest of shellfish.

• If you're harvesting your own shellfish, be sure to check with local authorities (town halls, departments of national resources or local governments) for any local concerns or special regulations.

Portion Size

The final factor to consider when purchasing or harvesting seafood is portion size. Personal appetites, budget, the waste factor and the type of seafood purchased all affect this decision. I generally recommend 6 to 8 ounces (170 to 224 g) of edible meat per person. This means if you are buying a fish steak or a fillet with minimal waste, 6 to 8 ounces (170 to 224 g) should easily suffice for each serving. If you are buying or catching whole snappers or groupers, on the other hand, you'll need quite a bit more—perhaps 1 pound (450 g) per person, as only about forty percent of the whole fish is edible. Very rich, oily fish tend to fill us up more quickly than lean fish, so the portion sizes can shrink to perhaps 5 or 6 ounces (142 or 170 g). As in virtually any cooking question, let your personal taste and experience be the ultimate guide.

Proper Handling of Seafood

Once you have purchased or caught your seafood, it is extremely important to handle it properly. Warmth and time are the enemies of top-quality seafood. Although I live only ten minutes from the seafood shop where I work, I always pack my seafood with ice or gel packs to keep it as cold as possible during the trip home. Once seafood is brought home, store it in the coldest part of your refrigerator (usually the bottom shelf) with a bag of ice or gel pack under the package. Try to eat any seafood within a day or two of bringing it home— the sooner, the better. If I have too much or don't have time to cook the fish, freezing is a good alternative.

It is far better to freeze quality fresh fish and to properly thaw and cook it at a later date, than it is to let fish age in your refrigerator and then cook poor-quality "fresh" fish. Proper freezing is very important. Home freezing of seafood should be for a relatively short term, perhaps only one to three months depending on species and freezer temperatures. Lean fish freeze more successfully for a longer time than do oily fish. It is never a good idea to refreeze thawed seafood.

My favorite way to freeze seafood is to glaze it first; this helps to prevent dehydration and freezer burn. Simply lay fresh seafood on a baking sheet and place in your freezer. After ten or fifteen minutes, dip the seafood in a bowl of cold water with just a pinch of sugar in it. Refreeze on the baking sheet, and repeat process two or three times. (The sugar helps keep the ice flexible in your freezer.) Finally, when the seafood has a thin glaze of ice covering it, wrap in plastic or butcher paper, or place in a plastic food-storage bag. Another way to freeze smaller fish is to put them in a clean, empty milk carton and cover with water before freezing.

Regardless of how you freeze your seafood, proper thawing is as important to retain quality as is proper freezing. Whenever possible, thaw your frozen seafood in the refrigerator. Microwaving, thawing at room temperature, and even cold-water thawing may allow harmful bacteria to grow and multiply; plus, these methods contribute to moisture loss, which diminishes quality.

Ecological and Ethical Concerns

There is one other somewhat controversial choice we need to make when purchasing seafood: whether to buy wild-caught or farm-raised seafood. Aquaculture, or fish farming, is becoming a larger and more important force in the seafood industry every year. Over thirty-five percent of the world's edible seafood is now produced by some form of aquafarming.

Farmed fish have certain inherent advantages and, unfortunately, some liabilities as well. On the plus side of the ledger, farmed seafood is consistently priced and available essentially without seasonal limitations. The quality and quantity of seafood can be readily manipulated by farming. The world

Aquaculture is a growing industry that provides farm-raised seafood of excellent quality.

production of salmon, for instance, has exploded over the last twenty years due to extensive aquaculture in Norway, Chile and many other countries. The price of salmon has precipitously dropped as production has increased, making salmon much more of an everyday food than it once could have been.

Additionally, since seafood can be harvested essentially "to order," quality can be tightly controlled. There are precious few wild fisheries that can consistently produce great-quality seafood 365 days per year, while most aquaculture operations can do just that. Fish farms can also take the pressure off of heavily fished or overfished species. Sturgeon, for instance, which have become more and more scarce in the wild, are now farm raised and produce some of the world's highest quality and most sustainable sources of caviar.

The negative aspects of fish farming are basically twofold. First, there can be and often are intrinsic, unavoidable differences in the flavor of farmed versus wild seafood. The flavor of a farm-raised Atlantic salmon, while very fine and consistent, could never approach that of a perfect, wild-caught Alaskan King salmon. The varied diet of the wild-caught King produces a depth of flavor that the farmed Atlantic will never attain due to its limited exercise and regimented diet.

Perhaps the biggest downside to aquaculture is the potentially negative environmental impact that careless or inefficient farming may have. There is growing concern that outdated "open pen" methods of salmon farming may increase pollution levels in the oceans surrounding these farms. The chance that farmed salmon could escape and perhaps genetically cross with wild stocks is another potential hazard the aquaculture industry must face. Recent advances in salmon farming, including computerized feeding and "closed pen" systems, could do much to alleviate the potential for negative environmental impact.

In conclusion, with the world's protein demands doubling every twenty years, aquaculture will play an increasingly important role in our food supply. The question is not whether we should continue to farm seafood, but rather, what the best methods are to continue to grow seafood in a sustainable and responsible manner.

Like aquaculture, commercial fishing raises some issues. Overfishing is a particularly thorny issue that does not easily lend itself to quick or sweeping generalizations. There are so many variables when it comes to fisheries conservation that it can be extremely confusing even for professionals to "do the right thing." Most everyone agrees that consistent and sustainable harvests are a must to ensure the future of commercial fishing as well as the health of the resource. What is not generally agreed upon is how we can ensure an equitable sharing of the resource for everyone, from sport anglers to commercial harvesters to consumers.

No fish illustrates this quandary better than swordfish. In the last few years there has been a movement, initiated by chefs on the East Coast, to stop serving swordfish, because statistics suggested that smaller and fewer fish were being landed on the East Coast of the United States. While this was undoubtedly true, over the very same time period swordfish stocks in the Pacific and in particular around New Zealand and Australia have risen steadily. Thus, it is not sufficient to merely look at individual populations; we must look further at identical or nearly identical species from other areas to get an accurate picture.

Ground fish (primarily haddock, cod and pollock) stocks in the Northeast Atlantic were by any measure drastically overfished beginning in the 1950s and continuing into the early 1980s. These stocks have just started to "come back" recently. On the other hand, stocks of Alaskan and Icelandic cod remained healthy and productive during the same time period.

Chilean seabass currently is the most controversial fish when it comes to the question of overfishing. Most people would agree that the sudden rise in popularity of Chilean seabass motivated commercial fishermen to harvest unsustainable and at times illegal amounts of fish. What was once (as recently as ten years ago) considered an inferior, tasteless fish suddenly became the darling of white-tablecloth restaurants; this sparked unprecedented growth in commercial fishing. As the price skyrocketed, demand gradually dropped and an equilibrium between supply and demand was reached. We now appear to be at legal and sustainable levels of Chilean seabass fishing, although time will tell.

Certain fisheries such as Pacific halibut and salmon have been successfully managed for decades and decades. A great example of this is the Copper River salmon fishery, which typically starts around May 15. The escapement of fish upstream is meticulously counted, and future harvest times are tied to the rate of escapement. The fishery may remain open anywhere from six to twenty-four hours at a time and from zero to three days per week depending on the health of the resource. Scientists have determined what escapement is necessary to ensure consistent production four to seven years down the road. This has enabled consumers to consistently enjoy one of the world's best-tasting fish year after year, while still allowing the resource to remain healthy and enabling commercial fisheries to maintain profitability.

There are many sources of information regarding the health of fisheries, ranging from popular magazines to web sites for environmental or industry concerns. Consumers who are concerned about the health of fisheries would do well to avail themselves of as wide a range of information as possible.

Commercial fishing trawlers supply first-rate seafood as well as promote conservation of the resource.

CHAPTER TWO

Your Own Fresh Catch

Nothing beats the excitement or the wonderful sense of achievement you get from catching, trapping or harvesting your own seafood. Whether you are fishing for halibut in Alaska, going after marlin in Hawaii or digging clams in Maine, the sensation of catching your own defies description. Having a safe, fun and rewarding experience and getting that spectacular catch home in great shape will ultimately decide how successful your "hunt" actually was. More than a few anglers have been profoundly disappointed by a poor fishing experience, or improper handling of the catch resulting in a mediocre meal hardly worth the effort and expense.

Fishing Boat Options

There are basically four ways to go about catching your own seafood. These include "going it alone," joining the gang on a large independently run party boat, fishing from a charter boat with a few other paying guests, and the ultimate in charter fishing: an intimately arranged personal guide-boat experience. Each of these has inherent advantages and some disadvantages as well.

The guide boat is a great alternative for neophyte fishermen. A guide boat is usually a smaller boat with a captain or guide who is responsible for taking as few as one angler or perhaps as many as four. This guide is usually very familiar with local fishing conditions and regulations and is able to provide guidance, equipment and expertise for a relatively high price. Guide boats typically offer a very personalized level of service and close supervision.

A charter boat is fairly similar to a guide boat, although usually the boat is larger and offers perhaps slightly less personalized attention. A charter boat may take up to eight anglers; the level of service is still quite high but perhaps not quite as

intense as with a guide boat. Since more people are sharing the boat and guide, the price is often more affordable than with a guide boat.

A party boat is a larger boat capable of holding up to 100 passengers. These boats provide significantly less personal attention than either a guide or charter boat. Party boats may provide gear, or you may be required to bring your own (even if gear is provided, you may wish to bring your own). They are usually a more economical choice, as the cost of the boat and crew is shared by many people. There is typically a larger crew to provide help, but complete beginners may have a hard time getting all the help they need.

Going it alone has many advantages, and some major potential problems as well. By renting your own boat and using your own equipment you can gain a sense of accomplishment and control that is difficult to match. You can go where you want, when you want, and you may do it for as long or short a time as you wish.

The potential disadvantages are the reverse side of the same coin. For example, you can go where you want, but because you may not know where the fish are at any given time it may be difficult to find what you are looking for. The safety and security of an expert guide may be missed as well. It may also take a large amount of time to gather the equipment and information you need, so actual time spent fishing or harvesting your seafood may be considerably less than with a guide.

If you do choose to strike out on your own, try to do as much research ahead of time as possible. Many of the best resources are free or very inexpensive. Local chambers of commerce, tourist offices and bait and tackle shops can be invaluable resources. Local fishermen also are usually more than happy to share their experiences with you, and since they live in the area they are familiar with most of the challenges you are likely to come up against.

Local seafood businesses can also be a great source for inexperienced anglers. A number of years ago I spent a fair amount of time in the Outer Banks of North Carolina with my family, and when my kids showed an interest in crabbing, a quick trip to a local scallop business proved to be very helpful. They told me where and when to go and even gave me bait for the crabs.

If you feel that some variety of party, charter or guide boat is what you're looking for, by all means take a trip to the docks before committing to a particular boat. Check out the condition of the boats, talk to the captain and, if possible, talk to passengers disembarking. Is the boat clean and well kept? Do the anglers seem happy? Perhaps most important, is the captain someone you'd enjoy spending a day or more with? Finally, make sure to clear up the issue of who owns the fish you catch. Many boats operate on the principle that the catch belongs to the boat so if you want to keep your catch or even part of your catch, make sure to discuss this before committing to a boat.

Handling Your Catch

Regardless of how you go about catching or harvesting your seafood, perhaps the biggest challenge comes after the catch: getting the seafood home in great condition. Even a couple of hours at 80°F (25°C) can turn perfectly beautiful fish into a poor-quality or even unwholesome dinner. Most fishermen are so focused on the hunt that the catch itself is often neglected. There is no substitute for proper handling of your catch and, unfortunately, much of this handling must be done within minutes of the harvest.

The first step after the landing of the fish should be to bleed the fish. Blood is an ideal growth medium for bacteria and as such should be removed as thoroughly and quickly as possible. I prefer to clip both gills with a knife or wire cutter directly after landing a fish. As the fish is still alive it will pump out most of its own blood rather quickly, usually within a few minutes.

Next, try to get rid of all "blood areas." These include the viscera and the gills. The viscera are easily removed by making a shallow cut from the anus all the way up to the lower jaw; care should be taken not to puncture the viscera as they can release acids which may burn the flesh of the fish. After slitting the belly in this manner, just reach your hand in and pull out all the innards.

To remove the gills you may reach in and pull each side out, or you may cut them out. Some larger fish have very strong gill structures as well as sharp gill rakers (the back side of the gills), so take care when removing them. I wear a pair of heavy rubber gloves when pulling gills. It's best to leave the dressed fish whole after cleaning, as this allows less surface area of the meat to be exposed to air, slowing deterioration.

Once the fish is rid of most of its blood the goal becomes to cool it as quickly as you can. Covering the fish with as much ice as possible, as quickly as possible, is the key. A fish loses 50 percent of its shelf life for every 5°F (2.5°C) above freezing. If you have access to saltwater ice, which is colder than freshwater ice, by all means use it. Allowing the water to drain is important, so a cooler with a drain at the bottom is a must.

If you won't be able to use your fish within a couple of days, I recommend freezing the fish as soon as possible, then thawing in the refrigerator when ready to cook.

Concerns for the Sport Angler

Whether you operate your own boat, or fish from a hired charter boat, there are some concerns you should know about. First and foremost it is important to educate yourself about some potential hazards. The most common of these are ciguatera and scombroid poisoning, parasites, and environmental contaminants.

• Ciguatera is a toxin produced by microorganisms living in tropical reefs. Larger fish that feed primarily in reefs can pose a hazard. Most commonly, ciguatera is found in grouper, barracuda, snapper and seabass. Symptoms can range from short term to relatively long term and may include itching, abdominal pain, nausea, diarrhea and convulsions.

There are several things you can do to minimize the risk of this relatively rare but potentially serious poisoning. The single best piece of advice is to stay away from coral reefs when fishing. Most of these fish are quite territorial; fish found in the reef area have very likely stayed and fed in these areas. Ciguatera tends to accumulate in the viscera, brains and eyes of a fish and less so in the flesh, so you can further minimize potential impact by staying away from fish liver or other viscera.

You can "super-chill" your catch by storing them on crushed ice. It's one way to keep your fish fresh, but they must be drained often. Keep the cooler lid tightly closed but keep the drain of the cooler open.

• Scombroid poisoning is primarily found in tuna, marlin, jacks, mackerels and mahi mahi. These fish, when exposed to temperatures of over 40°F (5°C) for several hours or longer, produce histamines that can cause allergic reactions such as rashes, difficulty in breathing and gastrointestinal problems. Scombroid poisoning is quite easily avoided by cooling fish to below 40°F (5°C) as quickly as possible, and keeping fish cold until preparing and serving.

• Parasites may be almost impossible to avoid. Nearly all species of fin fish are subject to the infiltration of parasites. Although the FDA maintains that the vast majority of fish are safe, some species such as cod, swordfish and wild salmon seem particularly prone to parasites. Proper cooking or freezing are the best controls you can use to protect yourself from problems with parasites. Dr. Thomas Deardorff

of the FDA recommends cooking fish until it is opaque, flaky and hot to the touch. An internal temperature over 140°F (60°C) is ideal. Freezing at 0°F (-18°C) or less for three to seven days, depending on the thickness of the fish, is another great safeguard. All fish to be consumed raw should be frozen first.

• Environmental contaminants to avoid include PCBs, mercury, pesticides and fertilizers. Here are three easy and effective ways you can minimize your exposure to them:

1. Avoid harvesting fish from sources near large industrial centers that may produce contaminants.

2. Check local and state guidelines and warnings limiting consumption of certain recreational-caught species.

3. Avoid eating viscera, skin and particularly fatty

areas of long-lived, predatory species such as swordfish and sharks. Many contaminants such as PCBs are fat soluble and tend to accumulate in skin and fatty areas such as the bellies of fish.

• One other area of sport fishing, which can be extremely enjoyable and easily accessible, is the sport harvesting or digging of shellfish. Digging clams and the sport harvesting of mussels and oysters is a very popular practice on both the Atlantic and Pacific coasts. This can be as simple as following the tide out and digging steamer clams, or as involved as placing open barrels over the homes of geoduck clams in the Pacific Northwest. No matter which method you use, the results can be very rewarding.

One simple caution is extremely important, however. All filter-feeding shellfish (primarily clams, mussels, oysters and scallops) may accumulate toxic dinoflagellates, potentially resulting in the very serious paralytic shellfish poisoning. This condition occurs throughout the world at different times and is usually referred to as a red tide. The symptoms of paralytic shellfish poisoning can include numbness, vomiting, cramps and even paralysis. They may persist up to several days and in rare cases can even induce death. Luckily this condition is easy to avoid. Local public health officials keep a strict eye on water conditions, testing constantly. A trip to city hall or a local chamber of commerce, or a visit to a related web site, directly before proceeding is all that is necessary to prevent any potential problems. Typically this monitoring is done daily and updated very frequently.

• Finally, make sure to discuss processing options for your fish with your guide before deciding what to do with that large, beautiful halibut. The yield from whole fish to steaks or fillets can vary considerably from species to species and is sometimes an unhappy surprise to the sport angler. For example, a 50-pound (22.5 kg) whole halibut will yield only about 20 to 25 pounds (9 to 11.5 kg) of ready-to-cook steaks or fillets. A large tuna has a similar yield (40 to 50 percent) while a snapper, grouper or seabass may only yield 30 to 40 percent of its weight in usable fillets.

You should be given a choice of how your catch is processed. Most commonly these options are freezing, refrigerating and smoking. You may wish to have your catch processed a variety of ways, keeping in mind the relatively short shelf life of even properly handled fresh fish. Refrigerated or iced fish generally are safe, wholesome and delicious for only a few days—perhaps a week at the most. Good-quality freezing can help extend the useful life of your catch dramatically—up to six months if properly wrapped and stored. Smoked fish is usually good for a week to ten days with proper refrigeration.

The longer you plan to keep your catch the more important proper storage becomes. For short-term freezing of less than a month, simply wrapping the fish well in plastic wrap or butcher paper will suffice. Longer-term freezer storage will greatly benefit first from glazing and finally from a double or even triple wrap in plastic or butcher paper. As with most aspects of chartering, proper communication is the key to your future enjoyment of your catch.

Overall, the vast majority of seafood is safe and wholesome. By following a few commonsense guidelines, you will generally avoid potential problems.

CHAPTER THREE

Fin Fish Basics

At one time or another, the cook who wants to prepare fish may face two dilemmas. The first is encountered at the fish market, where the cook, clutching a recipe for halibut, may be disappointed to discover that the price of halibut on that particular day puts it out of reach. Other beautiful and fresh fish is displayed at a more attractive price; what will work as a substitute? The second dilemma is almost the opposite, and is one that I have seen many times in the twenty years I have been teaching fish cookery. In this case, the cook has acquired a beautiful piece of fish—perhaps a less-common species for which there are few recipes available. What now?

Cooking Characteristics

With so much variety in our oceans, it becomes extremely helpful to classify or group fish by certain characteristics. There are three main criteria we need to look at to classify fish. Oil content is perhaps the most important criteria, as it will guide us to the most appropriate cooking methods. Flavor strength is not to be confused with "good" or "bad" quality fish. And texture is critical for proper handling while cooking.

• Oil content is key both for nutritional and practical cooking reasons. Generally speaking, the higher a fish's oil or fat content, the higher the percentage of beneficial omega-3 fatty acids. These polyunsaturated oils have been shown to lower triglyceride and cholesterol levels, reducing the risk of heart disease.

From a cooking point of view, the relationship of oil content to cooking method is quite simple: The higher the oil content of the fish, the hotter and more direct the cooking method can be. Leaner fish require more gentle cooking methods, and often need fat added during cooking. For example, very fat fish such as tuna, salmon or mackerel are best with high, direct-heat cooking methods such as pan searing, grilling, broiling or baking with minimal added cooking fat. Lean fish such as halibut, cod or flounder generally need added fat and more delicate cooking methods, such as sautéing, poaching or baking with oil or butter.

• The next characteristic to look at is flavor strength. Our oceans supply us with an immense palate of flavors, from robust to delicate. Matching these intrinsic qualities with proper seasoning enhances the natural flavor of the fish; mis-matching can destroy it.

Assertively flavored fish such as tuna, bluefish and salmon benefit from cooking with stronger, more acidic ingredients such as red wine, vinegar and mustard, and more assertive flavorings like garlic, rosemary, basil and various peppers. Conversely, milder, more delicate fish such as cod, halibut and flounder need subtler, milder treatment: mild herbs like dill, thyme or chervil and simple preparations such as sautéing with white wine, lemon juice and parsley.

Flavor strength is not to be confused with freshness (or a lack thereof). Any older, less-fresh fish will taste strong or "fishy," but here I am referring to fish that naturally have a full, clearly identifiable flavor. Salmon, for example, has a unique and distinctive taste that most people could easily recognize and identify. Halibut, on the other hand, while equally delicious, is much more delicate and lighter in flavor, and might be mistaken for flounder, cod or other lighter fish.

As always, personal taste should be the ultimate guide when choosing a preparation. I recall a student of mine who loved to fish for halibut. He didn't care for white wine, a common ingredient in halibut recipes, so he perfected a simple halibut sauté featuring red wine, shallots and butter. The moral of the story is that regardless of what any book tells you, the final guide should always be your personal taste.

• When we look at a fish's texture we are really asking how firm or flaky a fish is: Is it firm like marlin, swordfish or tuna, or is it flaky like cod, halibut or trout? Firmer fish tend to hold up well to high-heat, direct-cooking methods such as searing, grilling or stir-frying while flakier fish need more delicate treatment such as baking, poaching or sautéing. Below is a chart of some popular fish species, ranking their oil content, flavor strength and texture.

For more information, see the Appendix (page 120).

SALTWATER SPECIES: COOKING CHARACTERISTICS

OILY FISH

FIRM		FLAKY	
Milder	**Stronger**	**Milder**	**Stronger**
Cobia	Atlantic Salmon	Black Cod	Bluefish
Sturgeon	Barracuda	Chilean Seabass	Mackerel
Swordfish	Bonito		Shad
	King Salmon		Steelhead
	Shad Roe		
	Sockeye Salmon		
	Tuna		
	Yellowtail		

MODERATELY OILY FISH

FIRM		FLAKY	
Milder	**Stronger**	**Milder**	**Stronger**
Shark	Coho Salmon	Arctic Char	Pompano
	Marlin	Corbina	
		Redfish	
		Spotted Seatrout	
		Tautog	
		Weakfish	

LEAN FISH

FIRM		FLAKY	
Milder	**Stronger**	**Milder**	**Stronger**
Grouper	Snook	Atlantic Cod	Lingcod
Monkfish		Flounder	Red Snapper
		Haddock	Rockfish
		Halibut	Sheepshead
		John Dory	
		Orange Roughy	
		Porgy	
		Sand Bass	
		Skate	
		Striped Bass	
		Tripletail	

Judging Doneness

Once you have settled on a type of fish and a preparation method, your next step is determining how long to cook the fish. Timing is the area of seafood cookery that is most difficult for inexperienced cooks to understand, yet it is critical to your enjoyment of fish. Overcooking is the biggest problem; if you've ever had dry, tasteless fish at home or at a restaurant, chances are good that it was overcooked. Undercooking, while less common, can lead to serious health concerns. Gauging the proper "doneness" of fish is therefore critical to your safe enjoyment in eating it.

There are many different barometers used to gauge the doneness of fish. In my experience, the best and most accurate description of perfectly cooked fish is that it has just turned from translucent to opaque all the way through. You can check the doneness by looking at the center of the fish while it is cooking, gently separating the flesh of the fish with your fingers, knife or spatula. The fish is perfectly cooked at the moment the center of the thickest part of the fish has turned opaque.

Another easy and reliable guide to timing is known as the Canadian Method, which states that fish cooks in 8 to 10 minutes per inch (2.5 cm) of thickness. This timing guideline applies to broiling, frying, grilling and baking in a hot oven. Therefore, a one-inch-thick (2.5 cm) halibut filet baked in a 450°F (230°C) oven should be finished in 8 to 10 minutes.

One of the most common adages around is that fish is done when it flakes. While this is true, it is also unfortunately true that fish flakes even if it is severely overcooked. Since most of us have grown up with meat as our main protein source, we are accustomed to cooking times that may be hours long instead of the few minutes that fish requires. It may take some adjustment to get comfortable with fish cookery.

I often tell the story of a relative to whom I gave a beautiful halibut fillet, all ready for baking, complete with a fresh herb butter. Because she was an inexperienced seafood cook, I gave her instructions to bake the halibut at 450°F (230°C) for 8 minutes. A few days later I asked her how it was, and was surprised when she replied, "It tasted great but was a

No matter how you cook your fish, the key to success is serving the fish just as it's done to perfection.

After choosing a recipe, shop for the fish you need. If one species isn't available just choose another that matches in texture. Shown here (from top to bottom) are tuna, opah and salmon.

little dry." I asked her how she cooked it, and she said she had baked it for 45 minutes because she just didn't believe anything could cook in 8 minutes.

In recent years, fish that has been seared but is still quite rare has become extremely popular. Even sushi, once thought to be among the most exotic of foods, can now be found in such pedestrian places as baseball stadiums and convenience stores. I think it's great that so many of us are becoming more adventurous and open-minded, but this raises a red flag for me: There are potential health hazards when consuming undercooked or raw fish. Like most protein sources (and even some vegetables), fish may harbor parasites. This is completely natural and has no connection with the quality or freshness of the fish. The vast majority of parasites are harmless nuisances; however, a few can be harmful. The two ways to ensure your safety when consuming fish are to freeze the fish, or to cook it to an internal temperature of 140°F (60°C)—the temperature of perfectly cooked fish that is just opaque. All legitimate sushi bars (and fish merchants that sell "sashimi-grade" fish) freeze the fish before serving it raw. Thorough freezing in a home freezer may take four or five days, depending on temperature, to kill any potential parasites.

Putting It All Together

Once we break fish cookery down into its essential parts—oil content, flavor strength, texture and timing—it becomes easy to create great fish dinners. Let's take a look at some examples.

You've gone to the grocery store and found a beautiful piece of fresh flounder for dinner; now what? If you consult the chart on page 20, you will find it to be a lean, flaky and delicately flavored fish. Appropriate cooking methods for this type of fish include sautéing, frying or baking with herb oils or butters. Very simply, then, you might brush the flounder with olive oil, sprinkle with dill and bake in a 450°F (230°C) oven for 2 to 3 minutes for a quarter-inch-thick (.6 cm) flounder. In about 5 minutes you

have created the centerpiece for a simple, delicious baked flounder dinner.

Another example could be finding a great tuna steak at the seafood market. In this case you are dealing with an oily, firm-fleshed and full-flavored fish steak that is ¾ inch (1.9 cm) thick. Here you have a perfect fish for barbecuing with a simple marinade of garlic, mustard and lemon juice. You could grill this fish approximately 3 to 4 minutes per side and the sharp, acidic seasoning is a perfect match for your richly flavored tuna steak.

Whether you are fishing for your dinner or buying fish at your local fish market, let quality and your palate be your guide. Always remember that you can substitute fish with similar characteristics in any recipe. A great halibut recipe will be equally rewarding when prepared with flounder. Seared tuna pepper steak would be great whether you use tuna, opah or salmon. Even though your recipe calls for tuna, remember that dinner will be far better with great-quality swordfish than "over-the-hill" or mediocre tuna. I would much rather take home inexpensive but perfect rockfish than ridiculously priced halibut in January, when halibut is mostly out of season. As long as oil content, texture and flavor strength are similar, consider fish interchangeable and your enjoyment of cooking and eating fish can skyrocket.

In summary:

• The oilier the fish, the higher heat and more direct the cooking method.

• Stronger, more assertive tasting fish accepts stronger, more acidic seasoning.

• Flaky fish need more delicate cooking methods than do firmer, "steakier" fish.

• For most methods, cook fish for 8 to 10 minutes per inch (2.5 cm) of thickness.

• Cook with the skin side away from the heat source first (see page 119 for more information).

• Have fun with substitutions and experimentation. Top-quality fish and fresh ingredients equal a great-tasting meal.

CHAPTER FOUR

Shellfish Basics

For many people, shellfish are truly mysterious. Students of mine have often wondered who first decided one could safely and enjoyably consume such odd creatures. What a pity that such a healthy, great tasting and exotic food is so often ignored by the home cook; but the simple truth is that most consumers have no idea how to prepare shellfish.

It is easiest to look at each type of shellfish separately when deciding on appropriate preparation techniques. But before we look at individual species, it is helpful to first learn about some of the unique considerations for purchasing and handling shellfish.

Shellfish will live for a much longer time out of the water in cold-weather months than in warm ones. Most shellfish spawn when water temperatures become warm, and the shellfish temporarily loses much of its strength (and flavor, by the way) while concentrating on reproduction. A mussel harvested in January at Prince Edward Island might live for a week or more, but that same mussel taken in August might die within a couple of days because it was weaker to begin with. It's perfectly fine to purchase shellfish in summer; however, be prepared to use it quickly, ideally within a day or two.

Do not wash, clean or debeard shellfish until right before cooking them. I can't tell you how many people have called me to complain that their shellfish died before they had a chance to cook them. On further discussion, I learn that they washed the shellfish as soon as they got home. Remember that these are saltwater creatures; fresh water will eventually kill them.

Whenever possible, purchase untreated or "dry" shellfish. Most scallops and shrimp, as well as frozen lobster and crab, are now routinely "dipped" in a solution of tripolyphosphate. This preservative causes seafood, particularly scallops, to absorb water. Treated and soaked scallops (also called "wet") can absorb up to forty percent of their weight in added liquid. When you buy treated scallops, not only are you purchasing very expensive water, but flavor and ease of cooking are affected because the scallops leach water as soon as they hit your pan.

If you purchase already-shucked shellfish such as oysters, clams or mussels, always plan to cook it before serving; bacteria levels may become elevated as the shucked shellfish sit in the container, making them dangerous to consume raw. If you want to eat raw shellfish, purchase only live shellfish from reputable dealers who have proper certification.

One other potential health risk associated with shellfish, particularly sport-harvested shellfish, is "red tide." This is a naturally occurring algae bloom that renders molluscan shellfish (which are filter feeders) dangerous to consume. These algae blooms occur sporadically all around the world, more often in warm weather than in cold. State health departments do a great job of continually testing and monitoring commercial harvesting beds and aquaculture sites to ensure a safe, wholesome resource. All retail outlets that legally sell shellfish are required by law to have this certification on hand for ninety days. If you plan to harvest your own shellfish, be sure to check with local authorities for safety information.

Now that we've discussed some general guidelines, let's look at individual shellfish species to learn more about recommended preparation.

Oysters

Oysters on the half-shell are probably the most commonly consumed species of raw shellfish. Their fresh, briny sweetness is enjoyed all over the world. There is a huge variety of oysters that can range tremendously, both in terms of size and flavor. The diminutive Olympia oyster is barely as large as a nickel, while many Pacific oysters can grow to be 6 inches (15 cm) or more across. Flavor profiles vary considerably as well, from extremely briny to almost sweet, from sharply metallic to soft melon-like flavors. Like wines, oyster differences may be bold or quite subtle.

The most common ways to prepare oysters include raw, steamed, roasted, fried and stewed. Already-shucked oysters may be purchased for use in virtually any recipe except when they are to be eaten raw. Shucked oysters are easier to use when cooking, although freshly shucked oysters have a superior flavor. A good-quality live oyster should live at least several days in your home refrigerator, while shucked oysters should be consumed within a day or two. If you want to enjoy your oysters raw, please remember to shuck them no more than a couple of hours prior to serving, and to keep the oysters as cold as possible to minimize bacterial growth. Oysters cook very quickly; 3 to 5 minutes on high heat is usually sufficient.

SHUCKING OYSTERS

A heavy rubber glove or a thick, tough kitchen towel and a good-quality oyster knife are all you need to successfully shuck live oysters at home. An oyster knife has a short, 2- to 4-inch, dull, stiff blade that comes to a point.

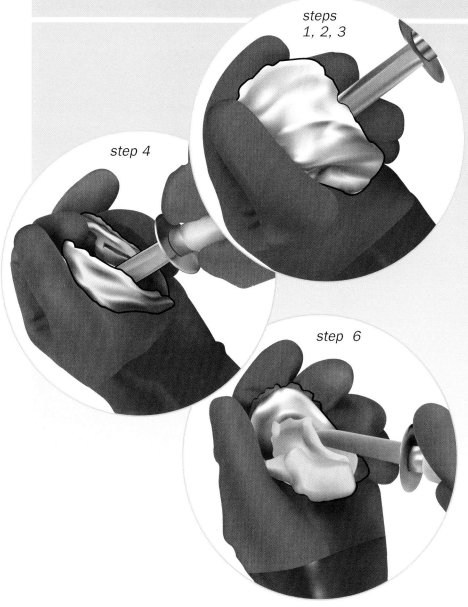

steps 1, 2, 3

step 4

step 6

1 Place the oyster, cupped side down, with the hinged end toward you inside the towel or in your glove.

2 Holding your hand firmly against the cutting board or table, puncture the oyster with the tip of the oyster knife into the tapered hinge end.

3 Turn your wrist to pry open the oyster.

4 Cut the oyster off the top of the shell by sliding the knife carefully against the top shell.

5 Pry off and discard the top shell.

6 Cut the oyster off the bottom shell and serve immediately, or refrigerate for an hour or two at the most.

Clams

With their special texture and sweet, salty flavor, clams are one of my absolute favorite shellfish. Steamed, raw, baked or fried, these delicious bivalves are both easy to prepare and wonderful at virtually any time of the year.

Probably the most commonly seen clams are members of the quahog family. These Atlantic clams are generally referred to by their size designations. From largest to smallest, these include cherrystone, topnecks, littlenecks and countnecks.

All of these hard-shell clams have a strong, briny flavor that is perfect for chowders or pastas, or eating raw on the half-shell. The smaller quahogs, littlenecks and countnecks, are somewhat more tender and less intensely salty than the larger cherrystones and topnecks.

Soft-shelled East Coast clams, or "steamers," are most commonly steamed open and simply served with their natural juices, or a touch of butter; they also make the world's best fried-clam dinner.

One of my favorite memories is digging steamers with my children in Maine. We spent three hours chasing the tide out, hunched over, carefully digging in the quicksand-like tidal beach hoping to pull out the succulent, delicate clams while avoiding the sharp stings of the blood worms. (These blood worms made their homes next to the clams, and at first glance looked very similar to our inexperienced eyes.) After back-breaking hours of pulling my kids out of the muck and digging at disappearing air holes, we harvested a meager 2 pounds (1 kg) of these delicious steamers, but their flavor and exquisiteness made the experience worthwhile. After this experience I vowed never to complain to my purveyors about clam prices again.

SHUCKING CLAMS

Shucking clams is very similar to shucking oysters. Instead of an oyster knife, however, you need to use a clam knife, which has a rounded tip and is thinner and slightly more flexible than an oyster knife. One side of a clam knife is usually slightly sharpened and thinner as well.

1 Place the clam with the hinge end toward you inside the towel or in your heavy rubber glove.

2 Wedge your hand firmly against the cutting board or table.

3 Using the thinner, sharper edge of the clam knife, work the knife gently back and forth all the way to the hinge, keeping your knife against the shell so you cut either over or under the meat.

4 Sever the adductor muscle holding the clam meat to the top and bottom of the shell, being careful to retain liquor in bottom shell.

5 Serve immediately or refrigerate for an hour or two at most.

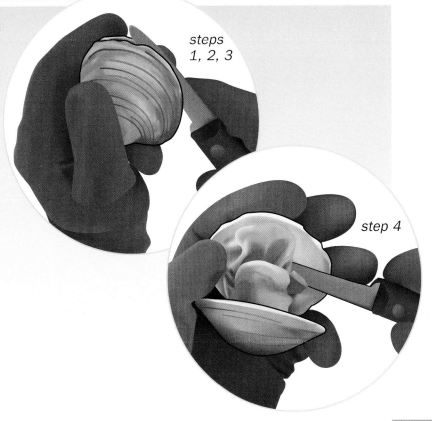

steps 1, 2, 3

step 4

The Pacific Ocean provides great clams as well, including the buttery, sweet Manila clam; the diminutive briny cockle; and the huge, bizarrely shaped geoduck (pronounced goo-e-duck). Manilas and cockles are perfect for a simple steamed-clam appetizer, and also taste great with pasta in a red or white sauce. The geoduck is beloved by sushi aficionados; these huge clams can weigh 7 to 8 pounds (3.2 to 3.6 kg) apiece, and sell for up to $100 each. The best, most tender part of a geoduck is the neck, which can extend a full foot (30 cm) outside the clam's shell.

Clams are more likely than any other shellfish to harbor sand in their shells and meats. Some people don't mind a little bit of grit in their clams, but if you do, there are two options to rid your clams of sand. The easiest way, in my experience, is to rinse and scrub them well, directly before cooking; after cooking, carefully and slowly pour off the delicious clam liquor, leaving the grit in the pan (almost like decanting an older bottle of wine). The other option is to purge the clams for several hours before cooking. This is accomplished by replicating ocean water with a solution of 1/2 cup (145 g) salt to 1 gallon (3.8 l) cold water. Next, add a handful of cornmeal and add the clams to the solution. Put this mixture into your refrigerator for 2 to 3 hours; the clams will absorb a little of the cornmeal and purge themselves of grit.

DEBEARDING MUSSELS

To remove the beard, simply tug gently from side to side until the beard pulls out; give the mussel a quick rinse and it's ready for cooking. If the beard breaks off, or you can't get it out, don't worry, as it is easy to remove after cooking.

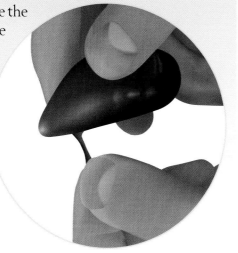

Mussels

The pedestrian mussel is one of the world's most underrated culinary treasures. Mussels are farm-raised virtually everywhere in the world, and are also harvested from the wild in many locations. They have not gone up in price in twenty years.

In North America, the farm-raised blue mussel from Prince Edward Island has become the dominant commercial force but greenlips from New Zealand, Mediterranean mussels from the Pacific Northwest, and wild blue mussels from the Atlantic are all readily available in most major markets (greenlips and Mediterranean mussels are generally farmed). You may consider all types of mussels interchangeable in any recipe.

Greenlips are the largest and meatiest mussel commonly sold. They have a deep, complex flavor and a rather assertive brininess. The Mediterranean has the advantage of spawning in the cold winter months, and is therefore at its peak quality just when the East Coast blue mussels are entering their weakened condition due to their summer spawn. The Mediterranean is a larger mussel with a great, rich flavor. The aquacultured Prince Edward Island mussel and the wild blue mussel from the Atlantic are virtually identical in size and flavor profile. Both are rather delicate and sweet, smaller and milder than their larger cousins.

Mussels are most frequently prepared by steaming, although they can be enjoyed baked or served raw on the half-shell just like a clam or oyster. Mussels have a beard, or byssus thread, that attaches the mussel to whatever it is growing on; these beards are heavier in worse weather, typically in winter months. Generally, the beard should be removed just prior to cooking. Some mussels also come complete with pea crabs inside; these tiny crabs are perfectly edible whole, as they are, or can be discarded.

Shrimp

Consistently at or near the top of the list of the most popular seafood items, shrimp is a quick, delicious, extremely versatile and increasingly affordable seafood choice. In all, there are more than 20,000 species of shrimp in the world and, while there are subtle differences, you should consider all shrimp interchangeable when cooking. Shrimp are almost always frozen and can be sold either as a thawed or still-frozen product. They are so perishable that truly fresh shrimp are a rarity for consumers unless they live virtually at the source.

The most commonly consumed shrimp in the United States are farm-raised tiger prawns, usually from the Far East (Thailand, Vietnam, India and Indonesia). These firm, delicious shrimp have become the dominant species because of the proliferation of aquaculture. The increasing supply and attractive pricing of these shrimp has made it easier for more people to regularly eat what once was only a special-occasion meal.

Other readily available species include white, brown and pink shrimp. These species are primarily caught in the United States, Central America and South America. The tiger shrimp has a firmer texture and slightly less sweetness than most white, brown or pink shrimp.

All shrimp are sold by the count per pound (450 g). Sizes can run the gamut from enormous 1- to 2-count-per-pound monsters, to tiny salad shrimp which may count out as many as 500 per pound. Bigger is not always better but is always more expensive, so consider trying a smaller size—say, a

16- to 20-count, or a 26- to 30-count—to save money. Almost without exception, smaller or larger shrimp may be substituted for one another in any recipe. Just keep in mind that smaller shrimp cook more quickly than larger varieties.

Based on your recipe and personal preference, shrimp may be cooked with or without their heads intact, with the shell on or shelled, and deveined or not. (The vein is part of the intestines and may be gritty or sandy, especially in larger shrimp. This grit is not harmful, but the vein is often removed for aesthetic reasons.) Most people find a peeled and deveined raw shrimp easiest to use.

Most shrimp dishes are very easy to prepare. Shrimp cook quickly; they may be boiled, steamed, grilled, baked or sautéed. They turn red while cooking regardless of their species, and should cook in 3 to 7 minutes depending on size and temperature.

Lobster

There are two main types of lobster available internationally: the cold-water lobster and the warm-water lobster. Cold-water species, such as Maine or Canadian lobsters, South African lobsters, and most lobsters from South and West Australia, are considered the premier species

PEELING & DEVEINING SHRIMP

1 Pinch off the head where it meets the body, reserving the heads for stock (page 105) if you wish.

2 a. Peel the shell off, starting with the legs and "belly" of the shrimp.
b. You may leave the tail and last section of shell on, if desired, for cosmetic purposes.

3 Run a paring knife down the back of the shrimp and gently pull out the vein.

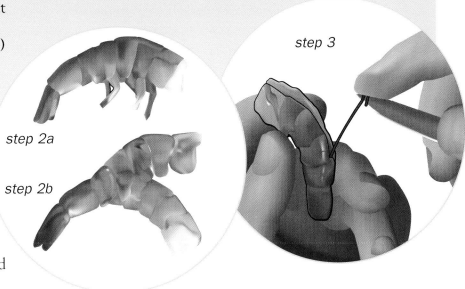

step 2a

step 2b

step 3

throughout the world. Warm-water lobsters most often come from Central America and South America, largely Brazil and Honduras. Most people find the cold-water lobsters to be sweeter and firmer than warm-water lobsters; however, both are outstanding and treasured luxuries.

Cold-water lobsters are sold exclusively as either live whole lobsters or frozen tails. Live cold-water lobsters have enzymes that begin to deteriorate the flesh in as little as 4 hours after death, rendering the meat mealy and soft. If you purchase a live lobster and it dies before you're ready to cook it, you may stretch the refrigerator shelf life by twisting off the claws and tail and discarding the lobster's body. With refrigeration, your lobster should hold up at least 24 hours this way. Cold-water lobster tails, while very expensive, are a great alternative to the touchy live lobster.

Warm-water lobsters are mostly sold as tails although sometimes, especially in areas that produce warm-water lobsters, they are available whole, either raw or cooked. Warm-water lobsters do not deteriorate after dying as quickly as cold-water ones do, and can be enjoyed even a day or two later if kept properly refrigerated.

Lobsters are most commonly steamed, boiled, baked or grilled and are truly one of the world's greatest culinary treats.

Crab

To my taste, no other shellfish has the extraordinary succulent, sweet flesh of a fresh crab at the peak of its season. Among the crabs usually found in our markets, the Dungeness, king and snow crabs are from the Pacific while the blue, rock and Jonah crabs are from the Atlantic.

Snow and king crabs are almost invariably sold as a cooked frozen leg, or as a cluster that includes a portion of the body as well as the legs and claws. King crabs are larger and have a slightly sweeter taste than the salty-sweet snow crab. Both of these crabs are sold in different sizes; large crabs are much more expensive than smaller crabs but also offer a larger yield or percentage of meat to shell. These crabs need only be steamed, boiled or baked to warm through, as they come fully cooked from

the boats. Most people enjoy these spectacular crabs simply served with melted butter or lemon.

Dungeness crabs, which are caught from northern California up through Alaska, are smaller than king or snow crabs, weighing an average of 1$\frac{1}{2}$ pounds (680 g) per crab. For conservation reasons, only male crabs are taken; they are sold primarily as cooked and ready-to-eat, or occasionally as live crabs ready to be boiled. Dungeness crabmeat is also picked and sold as a fresh or frozen product, primarily in the western United States. Dungeness have perhaps the sweetest, most flavorful meat of any crab and are most often simply served cracked and chilled, with lemon or mayonnaise. Quite a bit of the meat also finds its way into crab cakes at some of the best restaurants in the world. For some Asian dishes, Dungeness crabs are chopped into pieces and stir-fried with spices for an unbelievable treat.

I have fond memories of catching blue crabs in the Outer Banks of North Carolina. Although commercially trapped, these smallish crabs are incredibly easy to catch. Just lowering a chicken neck on a string into the water brought a teeming mass of angry crabs. We carefully brought these back to our cabin, boiled them with Old Bay Seasoning for 5 minutes and pounded, picked and ate for a half hour of the most delightful time I ever spent. Blue crabs are regularly sold as picked meat, ranging in size from jumbo lump down to the sweet, little gray claw meat. This meat is sold as fresh, frozen or pasteurized and can be used in almost any crab recipe. Live blue crabs also appear in fish markets, although they travel poorly and eat each other and so are difficult to get outside of the eastern United States.

From the early part of May until late September or even late October (depending on water temperature), blue crabs will molt, or lose their shells. Within 24 hours of losing their shells the crabs begin to form new, larger shells and resume eating to fill up these new homes. If you are lucky enough to catch, trap or purchase these soft-shell crabs you are in for one of the greatest treats. Dress a soft-shell or "shedder" crab as shown, and you will have a wonderful morsel ready to be simply floured and sautéed or grilled. Soft-shells are sold by size, ranging from a "whale" weighing approximately 6 ounces (170 g), down to a "hotel" weighing about 2 ounces (57 g).

Less widely known are the closely related rock and Jonah crabs of the North Atlantic. These smallish crabs, while relatively unknown west of the Mississippi, nonetheless provide very high quality, affordable crabmeat to many markets on the East Coast and Midwest. In recent years, this meat has been marketed as Peekytoe crabmeat. These crabs are almost exclusively commercially cooked and picked and are versatile enough for any recipe calling for crabmeat, often for half the price of blue or Dungeness crabmeat.

CLEANING SOFT-SHELL CRABS

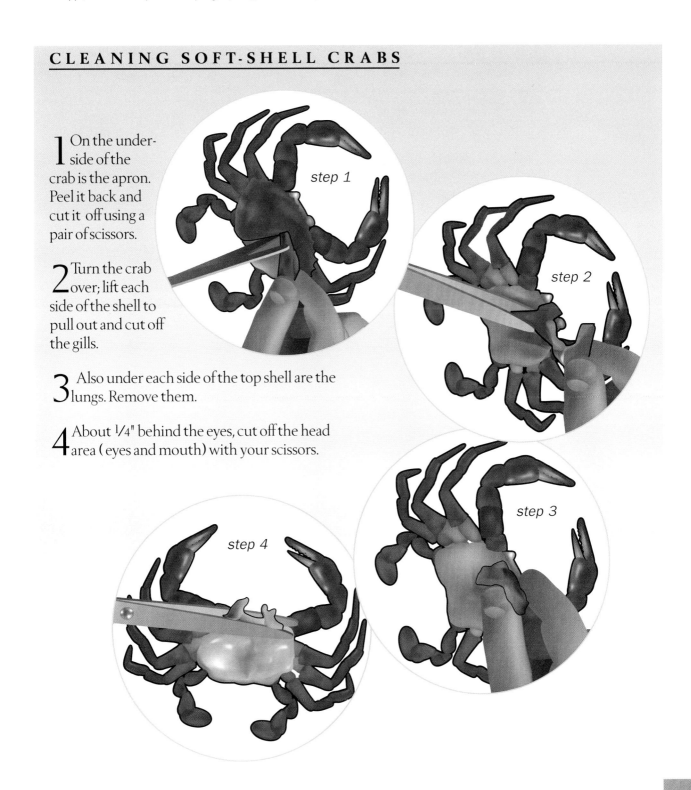

1 On the underside of the crab is the apron. Peel it back and cut it off using a pair of scissors.

2 Turn the crab over; lift each side of the shell to pull out and cut off the gills.

3 Also under each side of the top shell are the lungs. Remove them.

4 About 1/4" behind the eyes, cut off the head area (eyes and mouth) with your scissors.

step 1

step 2

step 3

step 4

Squid and Octopus

Many people do not realize that both squid and octopus are actually shellfish. Among the most underutilized seafood in the United States, these two are extremely popular in many parts of the world and are used quite extensively in many of the great cuisines.

Squid may be sold as whole (round) or cleaned, and may be fresh or frozen. Of these forms, frozen and cleaned is probably the most convenient to use. On the other hand, if you enjoy being wrist-deep in squid and squid ink as I do, or want to use the ink sac (also called sepia) in a recipe, by all means purchase whole squid and clean it yourself.

Cooking squid breaks all the commonly held rules for cooking seafood. There is a "2- or 20-minute" rule that works wonders. This method gives you two options for cooking squid. Cook the squid at high heat for less that 2 minutes, usually by stir-frying, grilling, deep frying or sautéing. Or, if you prefer, turn the heat down low, add a liquid and braise, poach or steam for 20 minutes or longer. Either method

will yield delicious, tender squid with absolutely no similarity to the rubber-band texture most of us associate with squid.

Octopus, a cephalopod like squid, can vary tremendously in size, from tiny baby octopus less than 1 inch (2.5 cm) in diameter to 100-pound (45 kg) monsters from the Pacific Northwest. Octopus can be purchased whole or just as tentacles, and may also be cooked or canned. Cooked octopus is also known as Tako, particularly in Asian recipes.

To clean octopus, simply cut off the head. The tentacles are ready for cooking as is, while the head can also be used once the viscera are removed. Slice the head into thin pieces or dice it. There are many theories as to how to tenderize the relatively tough octopus, ranging from beating to freezing. I have found that a long, mild simmer in water, wine or stock works best. After simmering for 30 to 60 minutes, depending on the size of the octopus, cool the octopus in ice water or in the refrigerator. Then slice or chop the octopus into desired sizes and the octopus is ready for any recipe.

By following a few guidelines, finding your own shellfish is an enjoyable outing and rewarding at the table.

CLEANING SQUID

1 Reach into the tube (also called the mantle) and gently pull on the head to separate the tube from the tentacles. Remove the ink sac (arrow) to reserve for use in cooking, if desired.

2 Remove the quill (or pen) from the tube. (When I first started cooking in restaurants I assumed this quill was packaging material and was amazed that each squid had such a simple, tidy package.)

3 Pull the wings and skin from the tube.

4 Rinse any remaining viscera from inside the tube with cold water.

5 Cut the head off right below the eyes, saving the tentacles and discarding the head and eyes.

6 Pinch out and discard the beak from the middle of the tentacles.

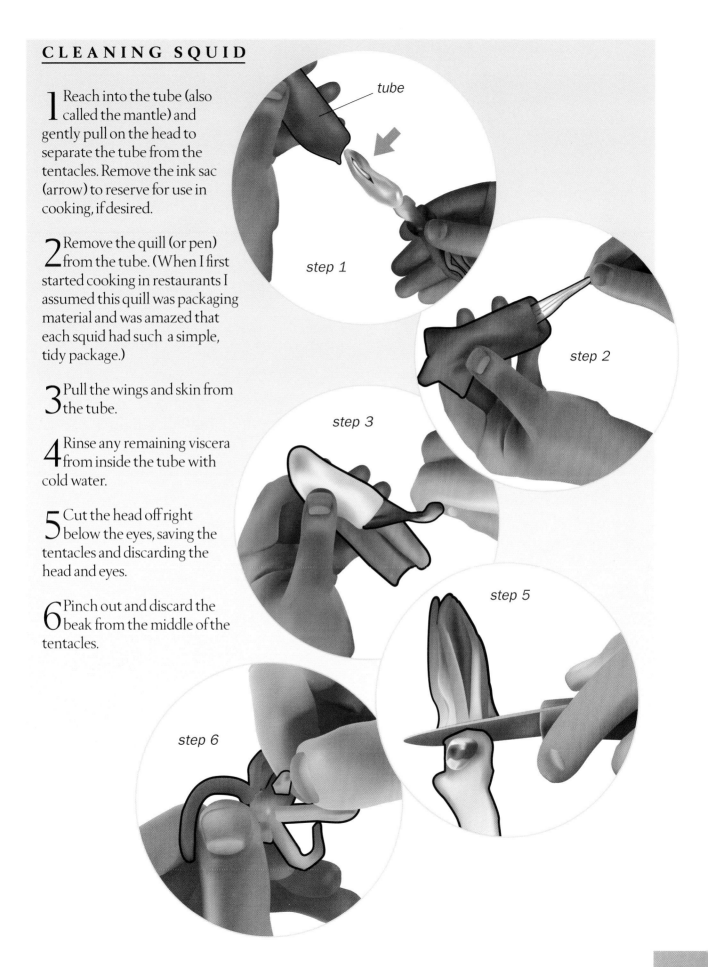

tube

step 1

step 2

step 3

step 5

step 6

CHAPTER FIVE

SMOKED SALMON CAKES

Breakfast & Brunch

Seafood for breakfast? Of course! Seafood takes center stage for an elegant—or even exotic—breakfast or brunch. For years I've seen my colleagues at restaurants and, more recently, our seafood business, start the day with a wonderful array of fresh seafood, ranging from raw oysters to seafood omelets to fabulous seafood casseroles. The light flavor of brilliantly fresh seafood makes a perfect start to a day, and the healthy profile of seafood only enhances the appeal of a breakfast or brunch centered on fresh seafood.

FRIED SHAD ROE WITH BACON

Serves 4 to 6
Preparation: Under 15 minutes

Shad are an anadromous fish that hatch in streams around both the Atlantic and Pacific Oceans. Every spring these fat, oily fish return to the streams to spawn, similar in many ways to salmon. Starting as early as February and continuing into May or June, shad and their roe have been enjoyed for hundreds of years. With a very complicated bone structure featuring three sets of floating pin bones, shad are almost impossible to bone (it's said that only a few people have the expertise to perform this task). In the past, Native Americans roasted shad on wooden planks over an open fire, hoping to dissolve the bones and make the fish easier to eat. In most markets now, the roe sacs—two lobes from each fish—are all that is commonly sold. Their rich, meaty flavor is perfectly enhanced by the smoky bacon and tart lemon juice in this recipe. This was often Sunday morning breakfast in my family, and was usually served with scrambled eggs on the side.

1/2 pound (225 g) good-quality, thick-sliced bacon cut into 1/2-inch (1.25 cm) pieces

1 cup (140 g) all-purpose flour

1 teaspoon (6 g) salt

1/2 teaspoon (1.25 g) pepper

2 pairs shad roe (4 to 6 ounces/ 113 to 170 g per pair)

1 lemon, cut in half

In large, heavy skillet fry bacon over medium heat until crisp. Transfer bacon to paper towel–lined bowl; set aside. Pour off all but 2 tablespoons (30 ml) of drippings, and return to medium heat. In shallow dish, combine flour, salt and pepper; stir to mix. Lightly dredge shad roe in flour mixture, and gently place in skillet. Fry until golden brown, 3 to 4 minutes per side. Squeeze lemon juice into skillet and serve with crisped bacon pieces on top.

SMOKED SALMON CAKES

Serves 4 to 6
Preparation: Over 1 hour; if potatoes are cooked in advance, final preparation is under 15 minutes

These delicious, smoky cakes taste almost like a hash. They're a perfect accompaniment to eggs for a hearty breakfast. To speed preparations in the morning, cook the potatoes the night before and refrigerate until needed.

3 large potatoes, peeled

1 onion, finely diced

1/2 cup (50 g) chopped green onions (white and green parts)

2 tablespoons (30 g) butter

8 ounces (225 g) hot-smoked salmon,* flaked

2 eggs

1 teaspoon (6 g) salt

1/2 teaspoon (1.25 g) white pepper

2 tablespoons (3 g) snipped fresh dill weed

3 tablespoons (45 ml) canola or other mild oil

Lemon or lime juice for serving, optional

In saucepan, cook potatoes in boiling water until tender, 30 to 40 minutes. Drain potatoes and mash or run through a food mill or ricer. Let potatoes cool for 30 to 60 minutes in refrigerator, or as long as overnight.

For final preparation: In medium skillet, sauté onion and green onions in butter over medium heat until soft; remove from heat. In large bowl, combine salmon, eggs, salt, pepper, dill and cooled potatoes. Mix gently, then add cooked onion mixture and mix again. Gently form into patties approximately 3 inches (7.5 cm) across and 1/2 inch (1.25 cm) thick.

Heat large skillet over medium heat and add canola oil. When oil is hot, gently add patties and fry for 3 minutes on each side. Serve as is, or with a squeeze of fresh lemon or lime juice.

*Hot-smoked salmon has been smoked at higher temperatures, and for a shorter time, than cold-smoked salmon. It generally is moister than cold-smoked salmon, and has a texture more like regular cooked fish. It is sometimes referred to as "smoke-cooked."

SHRIMP, MUSHROOM AND FRESH HERB OMELET

Serves 1 generously
Preparation: Under 30 minutes

1 small onion, diced

2 tablespoons (30 g) butter, divided

1/4 pound (113 g) mushrooms, trimmed and quartered

1/4 pound (113 g) peeled and deveined raw shrimp, cut into 1/2-inch (1.25 cm) pieces

1 tablespoon (2 to 4 g) minced fresh herbs (pick 1 or more of the following: dill, tarragon, thyme, basil, chervil)

3 eggs

Salt and pepper

Heat oven to 200°F (93°C) if you will be preparing more than 1 omelet. In small skillet over medium heat, sauté onion in 1 tablespoon (15 g) of the butter until soft and translucent. Add mushrooms and sauté until they give up their liquid. Add shrimp and herbs; sauté for about 2 minutes longer. Remove from heat; set aside and keep warm.

Place small nonstick skillet over medium-high heat. In small bowl, lightly beat eggs with salt and pepper to taste. When skillet is very hot, add remaining 1 tablespoon (15 g) of butter; as soon as foam subsides, pour egg mixture in all at once. Start stirring with a rubber or plastic spatula immediately. As soon as eggs start to set, stop stirring and spread egg mixture out to edges of skillet. Pour shrimp filling in a line along middle of eggs. Lift an edge of cooked egg up over filling, and roll omelet out onto a plate. Serve immediately, or keep warm in oven while you prepare additional omelets.

CRISPY PARMESAN OVEN-FRIED FISH FILLETS

Serves 6 to 8
Preparation: Under 30 minutes

1 tablespoon (15 ml) canola or other mild oil

1 egg

1/4 cup (60 ml) milk

1/2 cup (63 g) grated Parmesan cheese

1/2 cup (70 g) all-purpose flour

1 teaspoon (2 g) paprika

1/2 teaspoon (1 g) white pepper

1/4 teaspoon (1.5 g) salt

2 pounds (900 g) mild white fish fillets, such as halibut, sole or cod

2 tablespoons (30 g) butter, cut up

Heat oven to 475°F (245°C); brush baking sheet with oil. In small bowl, lightly beat egg and milk together. In separate bowl, stir together Parmesan cheese, flour, paprika, pepper and salt. Dip fish fillets in egg wash, then dredge in flour mixture. Lay fish fillets in single layer on prepared baking sheet. Top with dabs of butter and bake for 8 to 10 minutes, or until crispy and cooked through.

CRABMEAT CASSEROLE

Serves 4 to 6
Preparation: About 1 hour

1/4 cup (55 g/half of a stick) butter, divided

2 tablespoons (15 g) all-purpose flour

1 cup (2.3 dl) milk

1 cup (125 g) grated Parmesan cheese

1 tablespoon (1 g) dried tarragon, or 2 teaspoons (4 g) chopped fresh

1 tablespoon (5 g) paprika

Salt and white pepper

1 pound (454 g) crabmeat

1/2 cup (50 g) chopped green onions (white and green parts)

1/2 cup (55 g) breadcrumbs

Heat oven to 400°F (205°C). Grease medium casserole well; set aside. Melt half of the butter in heavy-bottomed medium saucepan over low heat. Whisk in flour and cook for 3 to 4 minutes, stirring constantly; this roux should not brown. Whisking constantly, slowly add milk and cook for 3 to 4 minutes longer. Remove from heat. Stir in Parmesan cheese, tarragon, paprika, and salt and pepper to taste. Gently fold in crabmeat and green onions; scrape into prepared casserole. Sprinkle top of casserole with breadcrumbs and dot with remaining 2 tablespoons (30 g) of butter. Bake for 30 minutes, or until lightly browned.

COLD OVEN-POACHED SALMON WITH CUCUMBER DILL SAUCE

Serves 6 to 8
Preparation: Over 1 hour

This is a great recipe for entertaining because it can all be done in advance. The sauce actually improves if it is made a day or two ahead. The salmon is great chilled or at room temperature.

2 pounds (900 g) skin-on or skinless salmon fillet, pin bones removed

1 cup (2.3 dl) fish stock (page 105), white wine or water

2 bay leaves

1 teaspoon (2 g) whole black peppercorns

1 cucumber, peeled, seeded and finely diced

1 cup (2.3 dl/155 g) mayonnaise

1 cup (2.3 dl/227 g) sour cream or yogurt

2 tablespoons (6.5 g) snipped fresh dill weed

2 tablespoons (30 g) Dijon mustard

2 shallots, minced

Juice of 1 lemon

Salt and pepper

Heat oven to 450°F (230°C). Place salmon fillet in baking dish that is large enough to hold fish in single layer. Pour fish stock, bay leaves and peppercorns around salmon fillet and cover loosely with aluminum foil. Bake for 10 minutes, or until just cooked through. Remove from oven, uncover and allow to cool for 15 or 20 minutes. Transfer entire dish to refrigerator, and chill for at least 1 hour.*

To prepare sauce: Combine cucumber, mayonnaise, sour cream, dill, mustard, shallots, lemon juice, and salt and pepper to taste in small bowl; stir to blend. Cover and refrigerate until needed. Serve sauce with salmon.

*You may prepare the salmon as much as a day in advance; pour off and discard poaching liquid after 1 or 2 hours, cover salmon tightly and return to refrigerator until needed.

CHAPTER SIX

Roast Asparagus with Smoked Salmon

38

Appetizers & Light Courses

I love using seafood as a first course, luncheon dish or light main course. The delicacy of most fish and shellfish makes it perfect for simpler preparations, while the huge variety of colors, flavors and textures opens up infinite possibilities. Most of the recipes in this section could be stretched into a lighter main course or served as is for a great beginning to a meal.

As with any seafood recipe, do not hesitate to customize these to fit your tastes or supply. If you are digging clams in Maine but love the idea of the Steamed Mussels with Grand Marnier and Saffron (page 48), just use your clams instead of mussels. If Steamed Clams with Ginger, Lime and Cilantro (page 39) sound great but you or your guests dislike cilantro, try substituting another herb instead.

STEAMED CLAMS WITH GINGER, LIME AND CILANTRO

Serves 4 to 6 as an appetizer, or 3 as a light entrée
Preparation: Under 30 minutes

This is one of my favorite appetizers, and works well with almost any type of clam. Add a crusty loaf of bread and a green salad and you have a delightful light main course.

2 shallots, chopped

2 tablespoons (30 g) minced fresh gingerroot

2 tablespoons (30 g) butter

2 cups (4.6 dl) fish stock (page 105) or white wine

Juice and zest from 2 limes

2 pounds (900 g) scrubbed clams

Half of a bunch of cilantro, chopped

In large skillet that has a tight-fitting lid, sauté shallots and gingerroot in butter over medium heat until soft. Add fish stock, lime juice and zest and heat to boiling. Gently add clams to skillet; cover tightly and steam just until clams open. Check your pan every couple of minutes and remove clams as they open, transferring to a dish and keeping warm. Discard any clams that haven't opened after about 5 minutes. When all clams have been transferred, remove skillet lid; increase heat to high and boil to reduce liquid by half. Add cilantro and continue boiling for about 1 minute longer. To serve, put clams in individual serving bowls and pour steaming liquid over them.

ROAST ASPARAGUS WITH SMOKED SALMON

Serves 4 to 6 as an appetizer or light lunch
Preparation: Under 30 minutes

This is a great spring or summer appetizer. The richness of the smoked salmon combines perfectly with the light tang of the mustard and vinegar. Very quick and flavorful, this could be served with some cheeses and fresh crusty bread for a perfect light lunch.

1 large bunch asparagus (about 1 pound/454 g)

2 tablespoons (30 ml) olive oil

2 tablespoons (30 ml) balsamic vinegar

DRESSING:

1/4 cup (60 ml) olive oil

2 tablespoons (30 ml) balsamic vinegar

1 tablespoon (15 g) Dijon mustard

Salt and pepper to taste

8 ounces (225 g) cold-smoked salmon, thinly sliced

Heat oven to 450°F (230°C). Cut or break off tough ends from asparagus. Arrange asparagus in single layer on baking sheet. Drizzle with oil and vinegar, turning to coat. Roast for 10 to 15 minutes, or until barely tender. Remove from oven and let asparagus cool to room temperature.

While asparagus is cooling, whisk together dressing ingredients in small bowl; set aside. Wrap smoked salmon around cooled asparagus, arranging in serving dish. Pour dressing over wrapped asparagus and serve at room temperature.

CHESAPEAKE BAY CRAB CAKES

Serves 4 to 6 as an appetizer
Preparation: Under 15 minutes

You can squeeze a fresh lemon over crab cakes, or serve with a sauce such as tartar (page 91) or remoulade (page 89). Any good-quality crabmeat will work for this dish, although I tend to use less expensive—but more flavorful—claw crabmeat instead of the much more expensive lump or jumbo lump.

1 egg

2 tablespoons (30 g) mayonnaise

1½ teaspoons (7 g) Dijon mustard

½ teaspoon (3 g) salt

½ teaspoon (1 g) ground black pepper

Pinch of cayenne pepper

1 pound (454 g) crabmeat

1 cup (110 g) breadcrumbs (approximate), divided

1 tablespoon (4 g) minced fresh parsley

3 tablespoons (45 g) butter or vegetable oil

In large bowl, whisk egg, mayonnaise, mustard, salt, black pepper and cayenne pepper until smooth. Add crabmeat, ½ cup (55 g) of the breadcrumbs and the parsley; stir gently to mix. Form mixture into 8 patties approximately ½ inch (1.25 cm) thick.

In large, heavy skillet, heat butter or oil over medium heat until butter stops foaming or oil shimmers. Dredge crab cakes with additional breadcrumbs and lay gently in hot skillet. Cook until first side is golden brown, 2 to 3 minutes; turn gently and cook until second side is golden brown.

OYSTERS ROCKEFELLER

Serves 4 to 6 as an appetizer
Preparation: Under 30 minutes

Do not rinse and shuck the oysters until you are ready to begin cooking; keep them in a mesh bag in the refrigerator until then, to keep them alive and fresh. Once you've shucked them, proceed immediately with the rest of the preparations.

24 fresh, live oysters

1 onion, finely diced

Half of a head of garlic, peeled and minced

6 tablespoons (40 g) finely diced fresh fennel stalks or celery

¼ cup (60 ml) olive oil or butter

1 package (10 ounces/285 g) frozen chopped spinach, defrosted and well drained; or 1 pound (454 g) fresh spinach, chopped

2 tablespoons (30 ml) Pernod (anise-flavored liquor), or juice of 1 lemon

1 tablespoon (1 g) dried basil or tarragon

Tabasco sauce to taste

Salt and pepper

1 cup (125 g) grated Parmesan cheese

Heat oven to 450°F (230°C). Rinse oysters well, then shuck (page 26), being careful to keep oysters and their liquor on the deeply cupped half shell. Arrange shucked oysters on baking sheet or oven-proof dish large enough to hold them in one tight layer. (Traditionally, some cooks put a layer of rock salt down first for cosmetic reasons and to help the oysters lie flat; feel free to do this if you like.)

In large, heavy skillet, sauté onion, garlic and fennel in oil over medium heat until vegetables are soft and translucent. Add spinach, Pernod, basil and Tabasco; continue cooking until liquid evaporates and spinach is cooked. Season with salt and pepper to taste. Top oysters with spinach mixture; sprinkle with grated Parmesan cheese. Bake for 8 to 10 minutes, or until edges become bubbly and oysters turn opaque.

SIMPLE STEAMED MUSSELS OR CLAMS

Serves 4 to 6 as an appetizer
Preparation: Under 15 minutes

This is a great starting place for many different shellfish recipes. Vary the dish by adding herbs such as rosemary, basil, bay leaves or thyme to the steaming liquid for added flavor; or use fruit juice in place of the fish stock (any citrus juice works particularly well).

1 cup (2.3 dl) fish stock (page 105), white wine or water

2 pounds (900 g) fresh, live mussels, scrubbed, beards removed (page 28), or scrubbed clams

3 cloves garlic, minced

In pot or skillet that has a tight-fitting lid and is large enough to hold shellfish in 1 or 2 layers, heat fish stock over high heat to boiling. Add shellfish and garlic. Cover tightly and steam just until until shellfish open. Check your pan every couple of minutes and remove shellfish as they open, transferring to a dish and keeping warm. Discard any mussels that haven't opened after about 5 minutes; larger clams may take as long as 8 minutes to open. To serve, put shellfish in individual serving bowls and pour steaming liquid over them.

OYSTERS ROCKEFELLER

MALAYSIAN SHRIMP FRITTERS

Serves 4 as an appetizer, or 2 as a light entrée
Preparation: Under 15 minutes

Serve these fritters plain, or with a squeeze of fresh lime juice.

SHRIMP MIXTURE:

1/2 pound (225 g) peeled and deveined raw shrimp, finely chopped

1/2 cup (70 g) rice flour*

1/4 cup (25 g) minced green onions (white and green parts)

2 tablespoons (5 g) minced cilantro

1 1/2 teaspoons (3 g) curry powder

1 teaspoon (3.7 g) baking powder

1 egg, beaten with 1/4 cup (60 ml) water

3 cloves garlic, minced

2 shallots, minced

1 tablespoon (15 ml) canola or other mild vegetable oil

In large mixing bowl, combine all shrimp-mixture ingredients. Mix gently but thoroughly by hand. Form into patties that are approximately 2 1/2 inches (6.25 cm) across and 1/2 inch (1.25 cm) thick. Heat large, heavy skillet over medium heat. Add oil and heat until shimmering. Carefully add shrimp patties. Cook for approximately 3 minutes per side, or until golden brown and cooked through. Serve hot or warm.

*RICE FLOUR CAN BE FOUND AT SPECIALTY ASIAN MARKETS. IT IS LIGHTER THAN REGULAR WHEAT FLOUR, AND MAKES THE FRITTERS MORE DELICATE. IF YOU CAN'T FIND RICE FLOUR, SUBSTITUTE CAKE FLOUR OR ALL-PURPOSE FLOUR.

BASIC BOILED SHRIMP

Serves 4 as an appetizer
Preparation: Under 30 minutes

Serve these simple boiled shrimp with melted butter, or with any sauce you prefer, for an extremely quick, popular starter.

2 quarts (1.9 l) water	**3 cloves garlic, smashed**
1 small onion, quartered	**1 tablespoon (6 g) peppercorns**
1 lemon, quartered	**1 teaspoon (2 g) mustard seed**
3 bay leaves	**1 pound (454 g) shell-on raw shrimp**

In a pot large enough to comfortably hold the shrimp and water, combine all ingredients except shrimp. Heat to boiling over high heat. Reduce heat to a simmer and allow to steep for 10 to 15 minutes.

Increase heat to high, and return to a rolling boil. Add shrimp and cook for 2 to 4 minutes, depending on the size of your shrimp. Pour shrimp and water mixture into a strainer and cool immediately with running cold water (or ice cubes if you prefer). The cooked shrimp may be served as is, or peeled and deveined for future use.

CRAB DUMPLINGS

Serves 6 to 8 as an appetizer
Preparation: Under 30 minutes

FILLING INGREDIENTS:

1 pound (454 g) crabmeat

1/2 cup (50 g) minced green onions (white and green parts)

2 tablespoons (30 ml) dark sesame oil

1 tablespoon (15 g) Asian chili-garlic paste, or hot bean paste

Half of a bunch of cilantro, chopped

3 cloves garlic, minced

1 small hot pepper, minced

1-inch (2.5 cm) piece fresh gingerroot, peeled and minced

Juice and zest from 2 limes

1 package (1 pound/454 g) wonton wrappers

Soy sauce or Asian dipping sauce as accompaniment

Begin heating a large pot of water (at least 2 quarts/1.9 l) over high heat; it will need to be boiling to cook the dumplings. In mixing bowl, combine all filling ingredients; mix gently but thoroughly. Place wonton wrappers, a few at a time, on work surface; lightly moisten edges with water. Spoon up about 2 teaspoons (10 ml) filling; form into a ball, gently squeezing to remove excess moisture. Place filling in center of wonton skin. Fold in half, forming a triangle; press edges tightly to seal. Bring 2 ends together, pinching to seal. Arrange filled dumplings in single layer on baking sheet as they are prepared. When all dumplings are prepared, use slotted spoon to gently transfer dumplings into boiling water. Simmer for 5 minutes. Use slotted spoon to gently lift and drain dumplings, transferring to serving dish. Serve with soy sauce or an Asian dipping sauce.

SQUID WITH RICH RED WINE SAUCE

Serves 6 to 8 as an appetizer, or 4 as a light entrée served over pasta
Preparation: Under 30 minutes

Serve this dish as an appetizer, or use it to top pasta or rice for a light main course. The sauce is at its best if you include the squid's "ink." This jet-black substance (found in the ink sac) is surprisingly mellow, adding only a mild squid flavor to the sauce. It is prized mainly for the rich black color it imparts to dishes.

2 pounds (900 g) fresh whole squid, or 1 pound (454 g) cleaned squid

¼ cup (60 ml) olive oil

1 large onion, diced

4 cloves garlic, minced

1 hot pepper, minced

1 cup (2.3 dl) dry red wine

1 cup (180 g) diced tomatoes

Ink sac reserved from cleaning whole squid, or 1 package squid ink,* optional

1 bunch flat-leaf (Italian) parsley, de-stemmed and chopped

2 tablespoons (30 g) butter

If using whole squid, clean according to the instructions on page 33, reserving the ink sac. Cut squid tentacles in half; cut tubes into rings. In large, heavy skillet, heat oil over medium heat. Add onion, garlic and hot pepper; sauté until just barely soft. Increase heat to high and add cut-up squid. Stir-fry for 2 minutes. Scrape squid mixture into bowl; set aside.

Add wine, tomatoes, and ink sac or purchased squid ink (if using) to pan. Continue cooking until reduced by two-thirds. Remove from heat. Add squid mixture, parsley and butter to skillet and continue stirring off heat until butter melts and mixture is well combined.

*If you use fresh, whole squid, it's easy to reserve the ink sac during cleaning (see page 33). You can also buy squid ink in small, shelf-stable envelopes, or as a fresh or frozen product, in gourmet or specialty seafood stores.

TUNA CARPACCIO WITH FRESH HERB MAYONNAISE

Serves 4 to 6 as an appetizer
Preparation: Under 15 minutes

This elegant appetizer is surprisingly easy to make. Use only extremely fresh tuna, and freeze for several days so it is safe to eat raw (see page 15); or, purchase frozen sashimi-grade tuna from a reliable vendor. The herb mayonnaise may be made up to a day in advance to simplify last-minute preparation.

HERB MAYONNAISE:

2 raw egg yolks (use yolks from commercially pasteurized eggs for safety)

2 tablespoons (5 to 8 g) minced fresh herbs (tarragon, dill, basil, or thyme all work equally well)

1 tablespoon (15 ml) lemon juice or balsamic vinegar

1 tablespoon (15 g) minced garlic

2 teaspoons (9 g) Dijon mustard

1 cup (2.3 dl) olive oil

Salt and pepper

1 pound (454 g) frozen sashimi-grade tuna, thawed in refrigerator

1 small red onion, peeled and very thinly sliced

To prepare mayonnaise: In food processor fitted with metal blade, combine egg yolks, herbs, lemon juice, garlic and mustard; process to blend. With processor running, slowly add oil through feed tube in a very thin stream until mixture thickens. Add salt and pepper to taste. If prepared in advance, cover tightly and refrigerate until needed.

To assemble Tuna Carpaccio: Slice tuna very thinly across the grain. Fan slices on a cold platter; garnish with onion and prepared mayonnaise.

SEAFOOD-STUFFED GRAPE LEAVES

Serves 4 to 6 as an appetizer
Preparation: Under 30 minutes

1 pound (454 g) firm, oily fish such as tuna, swordfish or marlin

1 jar (16 ounces/454 g) grape leaves, drained and rinsed well

1 rib fennel or celery, finely diced

1 tomato, peeled, seeded and diced

5 cloves garlic, minced

¼ cup (60 ml) dry white wine

1 tablespoon (15 g) Dijon mustard

¼ cup plus 2 tablespoons (90 ml) olive oil, divided

Heat oven to 450°F (230°C). Cut fish into small portions, 1 to 2 inches square and ½ inch thick (2.5 to 5 cm x 1.25 cm). Lay out grape leaves on work surface, overlapping 2 or 3 of them to accommodate the size of the fish being used. Combine fennel, tomato, garlic, wine, mustard and 2 tablespoons (30 ml) of the oil in small mixing bowl. Place 1 piece of fish in center of a group of grape leaves; top with a spoonful of fennel mixture. Fold grape leaves over fish and place stuffed grape leaves on baking sheet. Drizzle with remaining ¼ cup (60 ml) oil and bake for 8 to 10 minutes.

Tuna Carpaccio with Fresh Herb Mayonnaise

SALMON-PHYLLO WRAPS

Serves 8 as an appetizer, or 4 as a light entrée
Preparation: 30 to 60 minutes

This is an ideal party appetizer, since most of the work can be done in advance. Assemble it ahead of time and bake directly before serving, or bake ahead and serve at room temperature.

Juice and zest from 1 orange

2 tablespoons (6.5 g) snipped fresh dill weed

1 tablespoon (15 g) Dijon mustard

8 sheets phyllo dough (approximately half of a 1-pound/454 g package), thawed according to package directions

1/2 cup (110 g/1 stick) butter, melted

1/4 cup (28 g) ground or finely chopped walnuts

1 pound (454 g) boneless, skinless salmon fillet, cut into 8 equal pieces

Heat oven to 375°F (190°C) (unless you are preparing the wraps in advance for baking later). In small bowl, combine orange juice and zest, dill and mustard; stir to mix. Place a sheet of phyllo on a dry, flat work surface.* Brush with melted butter and sprinkle with walnuts. Cover with a second sheet of phyllo; brush with butter and sprinkle with walnuts. Repeat process until you have 4 layered sheets; the last sheet should be buttered but should not have nuts sprinkled on it. Cut stack of phyllo into 4 squares. Place 1 piece of salmon in center of each square; top with one-eighth of the mustard mixture. Fold phyllo over salmon and brush top with butter; arrange on baking sheet. Repeat with remaining ingredients. The wrapped salmon can be prepared up to this point and refrigerated, covered, for several hours; heat oven to 375°F (190°C) just before you are ready to bake.

To bake, place sheet of pastries in center of preheated oven and bake for approximately 10 minutes, or until golden brown.

*KEEP YOUR STACK OF PHYLLO SHEETS COVERED WITH A SLIGHTLY DAMP TOWEL TO PREVENT THEM FROM DRYING OUT WHILE YOU'RE WORKING WITH THE OTHERS.

CRAB DIP

Serves 6 to 8 generously as an appetizer
Preparation: Under 15 minutes

This is a great recipe for a party, as it actually improves in flavor if it is made a day or two ahead. Serve with crackers, croutons or raw vegetables to dip. I use claw crabmeat because it is the least expensive and most flavorful, but any good-quality crabmeat will do.

1 pound (454 g) cream cheese, softened	**3 tablespoons (45 g) mayonnaise**
1 medium onion, minced	**1 tablespoon (14 g) prepared horseradish**
1 red bell pepper, finely diced	**1 tablespoon (15 g) Dijon mustard**
1/2 cup (50 g) minced green onions (white and green parts)	**1 pound (454 g) crabmeat**

In mixing bowl, combine all ingredients except crabmeat. Stir with spatula or wooden spoon to mix well. Add crabmeat, and gently fold in. If prepared in advance, cover and refrigerate until serving.

SALMON AND SHRIMP MOUSSE

Serves 4 to 8 as an appetizer
Preparation: Over 1 hour

This delicious, richly flavored mousse may be served warm, room temperature or chilled. It's wonderful when accompanied by a sauce such as a fresh herb mayonnaise (page 44). Feel free to substitute different types of fish or shellfish; scallops make a particularly flavorful variation. Just make sure that the proportion of fish to the other ingredients stays the same.

1 tablespoon (15 g) softened butter, approximate

1/2 pound (225 g) boneless, skinless salmon*

1/2 pound (225 g) peeled and deveined raw shrimp*

2 eggs*

3 shallots, minced

3 tablespoons (7 to 12 g) minced fresh herbs (dill, basil, tarragon, thyme, or chervil work well)

1 1/2 teaspoons (9 g) salt

1/2 teaspoon (1 g) cayenne pepper

1/2 teaspoon (1 g) white pepper

1 1/2 cups (3.5 dl) heavy cream*

Heat oven to 400°F (205°C). Begin heating a pot of water (about 1 quart/.95 l) over high heat; it will need to be boiling when the mousse is ready to go into the oven. Generously butter a 1-quart (.95 l) mold; tear off a piece of foil large enough to cover the mold, and butter one side of the foil. Select a baking dish that is large enough to comfortably hold the mold.

Roughly chop the fish and shrimp and put in food processor fitted with metal blade. Pulse on-and-off for 5 to 10 seconds. Add eggs, shallots, herbs, salt, cayenne and white pepper and process until smooth, approximately 30 seconds. Add cream and process until smooth and well blended, about 30 seconds longer. Scrape mousse into prepared mold and cover tightly with buttered foil.

Place covered mold in baking dish, and set on oven rack. Carefully pour boiling water into baking dish to come halfway up sides of mold. Bake for 35 to 45 minutes, or until center tests done with toothpick. Remove mold from baking dish and set on cake-cooling rack. Allow mousse to cool for at least 20 minutes before unmolding and serving.

*FOR BEST RESULTS WHEN PROCESSING THE MIXTURE, THE FISH, SHELLFISH, EGGS AND CREAM SHOULD BE VERY COLD.

STIR-FRIED SCALLOPS WITH CHAMPAGNE AND GRAPEFRUIT

Serves 4 to 6 as an appetizer, or 2 or 3 as a
 light entrée
Preparation: Under 30 minutes

*This elegant dish makes a wonderful appetizer, and could
also be served on a bed of pasta or perhaps saffron rice
as a light main course.*

2 tablespoons (30 ml) canola or other mild oil

1 pound (454 g) bay or sea scallops

1/2 cup (1.2 dl) champagne

1/2 cup (1.2 dl) fish stock (page 105)

3 shallots, minced

1 bay leaf

**1 tablespoon (2.5 g) minced fresh thyme leaves,
 or 1 1/2 teaspoons (1.25 g) dried**

Juice and zest from 1 orange

1 grapefruit, peeled and sectioned

**2 tablespoons (8 g) chopped flat-leaf (Italian)
 parsley**

**1/4 cup (55 g/half of a stick) butter, cut into
 4 chunks**

Place large, heavy skillet on medium-high heat; add
oil and heat until oil shimmers. Add scallops; stir-fry
for 2 to 5 minutes, depending on size. Transfer scallops to dish and set aside. Add champagne, fish
stock, shallots, bay leaf, thyme, and orange juice
and zest; increase heat to high and cook, scraping
pan frequently, until liquid is reduced by three-
quarters. Add grapefruit sections, parsley and scallops; remove from heat. Add butter, a chunk at a
time, stirring after each addition until the butter
melts.

SKEWERED TERIYAKI SHRIMP

Serves 4 to 6 as an appetizer
Preparation: Under 30 minutes

*These tasty shrimp are great whether served hot or at room temperature. My 13-year-
old son invented this recipe while he was cooking samples at our seafood store.*

**1 pound (454 g) raw shrimp, peeled and deveined (any size from 16-20
 ct/pound to 31-35 ct/pound)**

Bamboo or metal skewers*

1 cup (2.3 dl) teriyaki sauce (purchased, or from recipe on page 90)

1/4 cup (60 ml) light sesame or peanut oil

Juice and zest from 2 lemons

1 hot pepper, finely minced

Heat oven to 450°F (230°C), or prepare grill. Skewer shrimp through tail and
head end, putting 4 to 8 on each skewer depending on size of shrimp used.
Arrange skewers in pan large enough to hold in a single layer. In mixing bowl,
combine remaining ingredients; pour mixture over shrimp skewers. Cover and
refrigerate for 20 minutes, turning after 10 minutes.

Drain and reserve marinade. Bake shrimp for 5 to 7 minutes, flipping halfway
through and basting with reserved marinade; or, grill for 4 to 6 minutes, flipping
halfway through and basting with reserved marinade. Serve on skewers, or
remove from skewers and transfer shrimp to serving bowl.

*IF USING BAMBOO SKEWERS FOR GRILLING, SOAK THEM IN COLD WATER FOR 30 MINUTES BEFORE
USING TO SKEWER SHRIMP.

STEAMED MUSSELS WITH GRAND MARNIER AND SAFFRON

Serves 4 as an appetizer, or 2 as a light entrée
Preparation: Under 30 minutes

1 cup (2.3 dl) white wine

4 shallots, minced

2 pounds (900 g) fresh, live mussels, scrubbed, beards removed (page 28)

1 teaspoon (.3 g) saffron threads

1 cup (2.3 dl) cream

1/4 cup (60 ml) Grand Marnier liqueur

3 tablespoons (12 g) chopped flat-leaf (Italian) parsley

2 tablespoons (30 g) butter, cut into pieces

In large skillet that has a tight-fitting lid, combine wine and shallots; heat to boiling over high heat. Add mussels; cover tightly and steam just until mussels open.
Check your pan every couple of minutes and remove mussels as they open, transferring to a dish and keeping warm. Discard any mussels that haven't opened
after about 5 minutes. When all mussels have been removed, add saffron to
cooking liquid; cook until liquid is reduced by about half. Add cream; cook until
reduced by one-third. Add Grand Marnier and parsley; cook for 1 minute longer.
Remove from heat and add butter, a chunk at a time, stirring after each addition
until the butter melts. Serve mussels in a bowl, covered with sauce.

Skewered Teriyaki Shrimp

CAJUN PAN-FRIED OYSTERS

Serves 4 to 6 as an appetizer, or 4 as sandwich
Preparation: Under 15 minutes

I generally purchase shucked oysters for this recipe but if you prefer, feel free to shuck your own. These delicious fried oysters may be served as is, accompanied perhaps by a cocktail sauce or tartar sauce. For a delightful luncheon, stuff them into a loaf of French bread for a great po'-boy sandwich.

FLOUR MIXTURE:

1 cup (140 g) all-purpose flour

1 teaspoon (6 g) salt

1/2 teaspoon (1 g) cayenne pepper

1/2 teaspoon (1 g) ground black pepper

1/2 teaspoon (.2 g) dried oregano

1/2 teaspoon (.4 g) dried thyme

1/2 teaspoon (.2 g) dried basil

1/2 teaspoon (1.2 g) onion powder

1 egg

1/2 cup (1.2 dl) milk

1 cup (160 g) cornmeal

1 cup (2.3 dl) canola or other mild oil

1 pound (454 g) shucked oysters

In mixing bowl, stir together flour-mixture ingredients. In another bowl, lightly beat egg and milk together. Pour cornmeal into a third bowl. Add oil to large, heavy skillet and place over medium heat. While oil is heating, drain oysters and pat dry. Dredge oysters in flour mixture, then dip into egg wash and finally roll in cornmeal. Add breaded oysters to hot oil and fry for 2 to 3 minutes per side or until golden brown. Serve hot.

FRIED HALIBUT CHEEKS WITH ASIAN DIPPING SAUCE

Serves 8 to 10 as an appetizer, or 4 as a light entrée
Preparation: Under 30 minutes

Halibut cheeks have the same wonderful sweet flavor that halibut fillets do, but with a texture more similar to a scallop than a fish fillet. Halibut cheeks are a spring and summer treat that is hard to match.

DIPPING SAUCE:

1 bunch green onions, finely chopped (white parts only)

1/4 cup (60 ml) soy sauce

2 tablespoons (30 ml) dark sesame oil

1 tablespoon (15 ml) lemon juice

1 tablespoon (15 ml) lime juice

1 tablespoon (12 g) sugar

1 teaspoon (5 g) minced fresh gingerroot

1 teaspoon (5 g) minced garlic

1/4 teaspoon (.5 g) cayenne pepper

1/2 cup (1.2 dl) canola or other mild oil

2 pounds (900 g) halibut cheeks

1/2 cup (70 g) cornstarch

In small saucepan, combine onions, soy sauce, sesame oil, lemon juice, lime juice, sugar, gingerroot, garlic and cayenne; heat to boiling over high heat. Boil for 1 minute, then remove from heat and set aside to cool. In large, heavy skillet, heat canola oil over medium heat. When oil is very hot but not quite smoking, dredge halibut cheeks in cornstarch; add to skillet and sauté for 3 to 4 minutes per side, depending on thickness. Arrange halibut cheeks on platter, drizzle a little of the dipping sauce over cheeks and serve remaining sauce on the side in a bowl.

CRAB-STUFFED MUSHROOMS

Serves 4 to 6 as an appetizer
Preparation: Under 30 minutes

8 large mushrooms

1 medium onion, diced

Half of a green bell pepper, finely diced

2 shallots, minced

1/4 cup (26 g) coarsely chopped walnuts or pecans

3 tablespoons (45 ml) olive oil

1/2 pound (225 g) crabmeat

2 tablespoons (10 g) minced fresh tarragon leaves, or 1 tablespoon (1 g) dried

1/2 cup (63 g) grated Parmesan cheese

Heat oven to 400°F (205°C). Remove stems from mushrooms; set caps aside. Chop mushroom stems coarsely. In large skillet, sauté mushroom stems, onion, pepper, shallots and nuts in oil until onion is soft and translucent. Remove from heat; add crabmeat and tarragon and stir gently. Stuff mushroom caps with crab mixture, placing in large baking dish. Top with Parmesan cheese and bake for 12 to 15 minutes.

SPICY SQUID FLOWERS

Serves 4 to 6 as an appetizer
Preparation: Under 30 minutes

Scoring squid is a great technique because it accomplishes two tasks at once. First, it tenderizes the squid by breaking up the long fibers. Second, it makes an attractive presentation because the scored squid curls and blooms into beautiful little "flowers" when cooked.

SAUCE:

2 tablespoons (30 ml) soy sauce

1 tablespoon (15 ml) rice vinegar

1 tablespoon (15 ml) Chinese black or brown vinegar*

1 tablespoon (12 g) sugar

1 tablespoon (15 g) Asian chili-garlic paste

1 pound (454 g) cleaned squid

1/4 cup (60 ml) dark sesame oil

1 bunch green onions, chopped (white and green parts)

3 tablespoons (45 g) minced fresh gingerroot

3 tablespoons (45 g) minced garlic

Combine all sauce ingredients in small bowl; stir to blend. Slit open squid bodies and lightly score inside of squid tubes at a 45° angle, in parallel lines about 1/2 inch (1.25 cm) apart; take care not to cut through squid. Turn tubes 90° and score once more, creating a diamond pattern. Cut tentacles in half across the length to yield 2 shorter halves, then cut each piece in half horizontally.

Heat oil in wok or large, heavy skillet over high heat until oil just begins to smoke. Add squid, green onions, gingerroot and garlic and stir-fry for 45 seconds. Add sauce mixture and stir-fry for about 1 minute longer.

*Substitute rice vinegar, malt vinegar or apple cider vinegar for the Chinese black vinegar if you can't find it.

GRILLED HERB-STUFFED SALMON

Main Courses

All around the world, seafood finds its way to center stage at dinner tables. From showy, elaborate meals like Curried Stuffed Lobster on the Grill (page 81) to 10-minute gems such as Fish Steaks Stuffed with Feta and Herbs (page 58), nothing beats seafood for healthy, delicious and convenient main courses. Take simple grilled or baked fish, add a steamed green vegetable and some roasted or boiled potatoes; what could be better or easier? It is still a wonder to me that seafood remains a mystery to so many people. Hopefully these easy-to-follow and quick-to-prepare recipes will motivate you to try more of our ocean's bounty. As always, let your taste and imagination guide you.

SZECHUAN BRAISED FISH

Serves 4 to 6
Preparation: Under 30 minutes

2 whole dressed, scaled snappers, groupers or seabass (1 to 2 pounds/454 to 900 g dressed weight each)

1/4 cup (60 ml) peanut or dark sesame oil, divided

1/4 cup (35 g) all-purpose flour

1/2 cup (50 g) minced green onions (white and green parts)

2 tablespoons (30 g) minced garlic

2 tablespoons (30 g) minced fresh gingerroot

1/2 cup (1.2 dl) water

2 tablespoons (30 ml) soy sauce

2 tablespoons (30 ml) sherry or rice wine

1 tablespoon (15 ml) Chinese brown vinegar*

1 tablespoon (15 g) Chinese hot bean paste

Cut diagonal slits into fish, about 1 inch (2.5 cm) apart and down to the bones. In wok or large, heavy skillet, heat 2 tablespoons (30 ml) of the oil over medium heat until oil just begins to smoke. Dredge fish in flour and fry for 3 to 4 minutes per side. Remove fish and pour out used oil. Return pan to heat and add remaining 2 tablespoons (30 ml) of the oil; heat briefly. Add green onions, garlic and gingerroot; stir-fry for 2 minutes. Add water, soy sauce, sherry, vinegar and bean paste, stirring to blend. Add fish and braise until cooked through, 3 to 4 minutes per side.

*Substitute rice vinegar, malt vinegar or apple cider vinegar for the Chinese brown vinegar if you can't find it.

GRILLED HERB-STUFFED SALMON

Serves 10
Preparation: 30 to 60 minutes

This is a beautiful party recipe. The salmon may be served whole, right off the grill; or if you prefer, carefully remove the skin and decorate the fish. The smoky flavor from the grill combines perfectly with the fresh salmon and herbs. The salmon can be served hot, warm or cold, based on your schedule and preference. Serve it plain, or accompanied by a side of Tartar Sauce (page 91) or Cucumber and Mustard Sauce (page 90).

1 bunch each of 2 to 4 of the following herbs: dill, cilantro, thyme, basil, rosemary, tarragon, oregano

5 shallots, roughly chopped

3 tablespoons (45 g) coarse mustard

1 whole dressed, skin-on salmon (4 to 6 pounds/ 1.8 to 2.7 kg dressed weight), boned but intact*

3 tablespoons (45 ml) olive oil

Prepare charcoal or gas grill. Roughly chop herbs and mix in medium bowl with shallots and mustard. Stuff salmon with herb mixture; close by securing with twisted foil strips (or tying with wet kitchen string). Brush fish generously with oil and grill for 10 to 15 minutes per side over low to medium heat, or until fish is just cooked through at the thickest part.

*Have your fishmonger bone out the salmon from the inside of the fish, leaving skin and flesh intact while removing the backbone, rib bones and pin bones. If you're handy with a knife and are preparing a fish you've caught, you can do this yourself, but it takes some practice, a very sharp fillet knife and a careful hand.

POMPANO IN PARCHMENT

Serves 4
Preparation: Under 30 minutes

1 onion, finely diced

1/4 cup (60 ml) olive oil

1/2 pound (225 g) mushrooms, sliced

2 tablespoons (30 ml) lemon juice

2 tablespoons (30 ml) white wine

2 tablespoons (10 g) minced fresh tarragon, basil or thyme

1 tablespoon (10 g) drained capers, crushed

4 sheets kitchen parchment paper, 18 inches (46 cm) long

4 whole dressed pompano (about 1 pound/454 g dressed weight each)

Heat oven to 450°F (230°C). In large skillet, sauté onion in oil over medium heat until barely soft. Add mushrooms; sauté for 2 minutes longer. Add lemon juice, wine, herbs and capers; sauté for about 1 minute longer. Remove from heat.

For each serving, fold parchment paper in half; open again and place 1 fish on bottom half, about 1 inch (2.5 cm) from crease. Top each fish portion with equal portions of the mushroom mixture. Enclose fish in parchment with a series of overlapping folds (see illustrations on page 65, Fish Fillets Baked in Parchment). Place packets in single layer on baking sheet. Bake for 10 to 12 minutes, until pompano is cooked through and parchment paper is puffed up and brown.

WHOLE FISH BAKED WITH MUSTARD, ROSEMARY AND GARLIC

Serves 4 to 6
Preparation: Under 30 minutes

In many countries, whole fish is the only form commonly served. Whole fish are not only beautiful but often have more flavor than fish fillets.

2 whole dressed, scaled snappers, groupers or porgies (1 1/2 to 2 pounds/ 680 to 900 g dressed weight each)

12 sprigs fresh rosemary

4 cloves garlic, peeled and thinly sliced

2 tablespoons (30 g) honey mustard

1 cup (2.3 dl) dry white wine or fish stock (page 105)

1/4 cup (60 ml) olive oil

Heat oven to 425°F (220°C). Cut 3 diagonal slits on each side of fish, equally spaced and down to the bones. Stuff each slit with a sprig of rosemary, several slices of garlic and some of the mustard. Place in shallow baking dish. Pour wine and oil over fish. Bake for 10 to 14 minutes, depending on thickness of fish; fish should be just cooked through at thickest part.

NOTE: THIS EASY RECIPE WORKS EQUALLY WELL ON A CHARCOAL OR A GAS GRILL. SIMPLY RUB STUFFED FISH WITH OIL AND PLACE DIRECTLY ON GRATE; COOK FOR 5 TO 7 MINUTES PER SIDE (OMIT THE WHITE WINE).

MEXICAN REDFISH WITH CILANTRO

Serves 4
Preparation: 1 hour marinating, plus about 20 minutes cooking time

1/2 cup (1.2 dl) olive oil

1/4 cup (60 ml) lime juice

1/4 cup (60 ml) orange juice

1 large bunch cilantro, chopped

4 cloves garlic, chopped

1 teaspoon (.3 g) dried oregano

1 teaspoon (6 g) salt

1/2 teaspoon (1 g) pepper

1 whole dressed, scaled redfish or seabass (3 to 4 pounds/1.36 to 1.8 kg dressed weight)

In small bowl, whisk together oil, lime juice, orange juice, cilantro, garlic, oregano, salt and pepper. Cut 5 or 6 diagonal slits on each side of fish, equally spaced and down to the bones. Place fish in large baking dish; pour juice mixture over fish. Cover with foil and refrigerate for 1 hour, turning fish over halfway through; near end of marinating time, heat oven to 450°F (230°C). Place covered dish in oven and bake for 18 to 20 minutes, or until flesh is opaque all the way through to the bone.

Whole Fish Baked with Mustard, Rosemary and Garlic

Peppered Tuna Steak

ASIAN STEAMED WHOLE FLOUNDER

Serves 4
Preparation: Under 30 minutes

1 onion, julienned

2 whole dressed, scaled flounder (about 1½ pounds/680 g dressed weight each)

1 bunch green onions, chopped (white parts only)

3 tablespoons (45 ml) soy sauce

3 tablespoons (45 ml) dry sherry

3 tablespoons (45 ml) dark sesame oil

3 tablespoons (45 ml) orange juice

3 tablespoons (45 g) minced fresh gingerroot

2 tablespoons (30 g) minced garlic

½ teaspoon (1 g) ground Szechuan peppercorns

Place julienned onion in skillet large enough to hold both fish. Place fish on top of onion, head to tail so they fit snugly in single layer. Whisk together green onions, soy sauce, sherry, sesame oil, orange juice, gingerroot, garlic and Szechuan pepper; pour over fish. Cover skillet tightly and place over high heat. When liquid comes to a boil, reduce heat to low and steam, covered, for 6 minutes, or until fish are cooked through. Serve either whole or filleted, with steaming liquid on top.

STEAMED STRIPER WITH SCALLOPS AND HERBS

Serves 4
Preparation: 15 to 30 minutes

2 whole dressed striped bass (1 to 2 pounds/454 to 900 g dressed weight each), boned but intact*

2 tablespoons (6.5 g) snipped fresh dill weed

2 tablespoons (13 g) minced green onions (white and green parts)

2 tablespoons (20 g) minced red bell peppers

½ pound (225 g) sea scallops, thinly sliced

Juice and zest from 1 lemon

2 cups (4.6 dl) white wine or fish stock (page 105)

Place bass on steaming rack, opened up and skin side down. Arrange dill, onions, peppers and scallops over opened bass. Sprinkle lemon juice and zest over scallops. Pour wine into bottom of steamer; place rack over steamer and cover tightly. Heat to boiling over high heat; steam until fish and scallops are just cooked through, 8 to 10 minutes. Remove rack; continue cooking liquid until reduced by three-quarters. Pour reduced sauce over fish and serve.

*HAVE YOUR FISHMONGER BONE OUT THE BASS FROM THE INSIDE OF THE FISH, LEAVING SKIN AND FLESH INTACT WHILE REMOVING THE BACKBONE, RIB BONES AND PIN BONES. IF YOU'RE HANDY WITH A KNIFE AND ARE PREPARING FISH YOU'VE CAUGHT, YOU CAN DO THIS YOURSELF, BUT IT TAKES SOME PRACTICE, A VERY SHARP FILLET KNIFE AND A CAREFUL HAND.

PEPPERED TUNA STEAK

Serves 4
Preparation: Under 15 minutes

Fresh tuna has a taste and texture that reminds many people of beef, especially when prepared as it is here. I've offered samples of this dish at farmers' markets, and have actually had people argue with me that it couldn't possibly be fish they were eating. A tuna purveyor in Florida told me that after his mother's doctor told her to stop eating red meat, he served grilled tuna to her one evening. Her response? "But I'm not supposed to eat beef anymore!"

4 tuna steaks or other firm, meaty fish steaks, approximately ¾ inch (1.9 cm) thick (6 to 8 ounces/170 to 225 g each)

Coarsely ground black pepper

Kosher salt

1 tablespoon (15 ml) olive oil

½ cup (1.2 dl) dry red wine

2 tablespoons (30 g) minced garlic

1 tablespoon (15 ml) balsamic vinegar

Juice from 1 orange

Liberally cover tuna steaks on both sides with pepper and salt, pressing into flesh. In large, heavy skillet, heat oil over high heat until shimmering. Add tuna steaks and sear for 3 to 4 minutes on each side. Remove tuna from skillet, reduce heat to low, and add wine, garlic, vinegar and orange juice, scraping to loosen browned bits. Cook until mixture is thick and syrupy, 3 to 4 minutes. Return tuna to skillet and cook for 1 to 2 minutes, turning once.

HAZELNUT STRIPED BASS

Serves 4
Preparation: Under 30 minutes

1/2 cup (67.5 g) whole hazelnuts

2 tablespoons (30 ml) olive oil

4 boneless, skinless striped bass fillets (6 to 8 ounces/170 to 225 g each)

1/4 cup (35 g) all-purpose flour

Juice of 1 lemon

1/4 cup (15 g) chopped flat-leaf (Italian) parsley

Salt and pepper

Toast and peel hazelnuts as described below.

In same skillet used to toast hazelnuts, heat oil over medium heat. Meanwhile, dredge fillets in flour, shaking off excess. Add fillets to hot oil; cook for 3 to 4 minutes per side, or until golden brown. Transfer fillets to platter; set aside and keep warm. Add chopped hazelnuts, lemon juice and parsley to skillet; cook for 15 to 20 seconds, stirring constantly. Remove from heat; add salt and pepper to taste. Pour sauce over fillets and serve immediately.

HOW TO TOAST AND PEEL HAZELNUTS

1. In large, heavy skillet, toast hazelnuts over medium heat, stirring constantly, until fragrant and lightly browned.

2. Remove from heat; transfer hazelnuts to dish to cool.

3. Rub skins off with coarse towel.

4. Place skinned nuts in food processor fitted with metal blade; pulse on-and-off a few times to chop coarsely.

FISH STEAKS STUFFED WITH FETA AND HERBS

Serves 4
Preparation: Under 15 minutes

My 11-year-old son combined two of his favorite foods—meaty fish and feta cheese—to invent this dish in a cooking class. Unbelievably quick and easy, this dish is great for a spring or summer dinner. Swordfish or tuna are excellent substitutes for the marlin.

4 marlin steaks or other firm, meaty fish steaks, approximately 3/4 inch (1.9 cm) thick (6 to 8 ounces/170 to 225 g each)

8 ounces (225 g) Greek feta cheese, crumbled

2 tablespoons (6.5 g) snipped fresh dill weed

2 tablespoons (10 g) minced fresh oregano, or 1 tablespoon (1 g) dried

1 tablespoon (15 ml) olive oil

Prepare charcoal or gas grill. Carefully cut a pocket in the middle of the fish steaks. In small bowl, combine feta, dill and oregano; mix gently. Stuff cheese mixture into pockets in fish steaks; brush steaks with oil. Place on grate over prepared coals and grill for 4 to 5 minutes per side, or until cooked through.

FISH STEAK MISOYAKI

Serves 4
Preparation: 1 to 2 hours marinating, plus less than 15 minutes cooking time

If you prefer, cook the fish steaks on the grill rather than in a skillet.

1/2 cup (140 g) white miso paste*

2 tablespoons (30 ml) sake (Japanese rice wine)

1 tablespoon (12 g) sugar

1 tablespoon (15 g) minced fresh gingerroot

4 tuna steaks or other firm, meaty fish steaks, approximately 3/4 inch (1.9 cm) thick (6 to 8 ounces/170 to 225 g each)

1 tablespoon (15 ml) canola or other mild oil

In medium bowl, combine miso, sake, sugar and gingerroot; mix well. Slather paste onto both sides of tuna steaks and marinate in refrigerator for 1 to 2 hours, or as long as 24 hours (the longer you marinate the fish, the more the miso flavor comes through). To cook, heat oil in large, heavy skillet over medium-high heat; meanwhile, brush marinade from tuna steaks. When oil is hot, add tuna steaks; sear for 3 to 4 minutes on each side, or until desired doneness.

*Miso is a salty soybean-based paste that is a staple in Japanese cooking. Look for it in natural-foods stores or Asian markets. There are several types of miso; for this recipe, choose white miso, which is milder than the red or brown varieties. Miso keeps well, and can be stored in the refrigerator for several months.

Fish Steaks Stuffed with Feta and Herbs

GRILLED SWORDFISH WITH CHILI, GARLIC AND GINGER SAUCE

THE SALTWATER COOKBOOK

GRILLED SWORDFISH WITH CHILI, GARLIC AND GINGER SAUCE

Serves 4 to 6
Preparation: 30 to 60 minutes

MARINADE:

Juice from 1 lemon

1/4 cup (60 ml) soy sauce

1/4 cup (60 ml) honey

2 tablespoons (30 g) Asian chili-garlic paste

2 tablespoons (30 g) minced fresh gingerroot

1 teaspoon (2 g) ground black pepper

3 cloves garlic, minced

1 1/2 pounds (680 g) swordfish steaks or substitute, approximately 3/4 inch (1.9 cm) thick

2 tablespoons (30 ml) peanut or light sesame oil

In small bowl, stir together all marinade ingredients. Arrange swordfish in dish. Pour marinade over, turning to coat. Cover and refrigerate for 30 to 45 minutes, turning once.

Prepare charcoal or gas grill. Remove fish from marinade and brush on both sides with oil. Place on grate over prepared coals and grill for 3 to 4 minutes per side, or until cooked through.

CUBAN FISH WITH ALMOND AND GARLIC SAUCE

Serves 4 to 6
Preparation: Under 30 minutes

1/2 cup (70 g) all-purpose flour

1 tablespoon (5 g) paprika

Salt and pepper

3 tablespoons (45 ml) olive oil

1 1/2 to 2 pounds (680 to 900 g) mild flaky fish fillets, such as halibut, cod or haddock

2 onions, sliced

Half of a head of garlic, peeled and minced

1 cup (140 g) whole almonds, toasted then ground (about 1/2 cup/ 70 g ground almonds

Juice and zest from 2 limes

2 bay leaves

1 cup (2.3 dl) dry white wine

1 cup (2.3 dl) fish stock (page 105)

1/4 cup (15 g) chopped flat-leaf (Italian) parsley

Mix flour, paprika, and salt and pepper to taste in bowl. Place large, heavy skillet over medium-high heat; when skillet is hot, add oil. Dredge fish in flour mixture. Add to skillet and fry until brown on both sides, 2 to 3 minutes per side. Transfer fish to plate and set aside.

Add onions, garlic and almonds to skillet; sauté over medium heat for 3 to 4 minutes, or until onions and garlic are soft but not too brown. Add lime juice and zest, bay leaves, wine and fish stock. Increase heat to high and cook until reduced by three-quarters. Add parsley and fish and continue cooking until fish is just cooked through, 2 to 3 minutes.

SPICED FISH WITH TAMARIND AND COCONUT

Serves 4 to 6
Preparation: About 1 hour

MARINADE:

3 cloves garlic, minced

Juice and zest from 2 limes

2 pounds (900 g) boneless, skinless red snapper or grouper fillets

1/4 cup (60 ml) canola or other mild oil

1/4 cup (35 g) all-purpose flour

1 large onion, julienned

3 cloves garlic, minced

1 cup (2.3 dl) coconut milk

3 bay leaves

3 tablespoons (40 g) tamarind paste*

1 tablespoon (5 g) hot paprika

1 teaspoon (.75 g) dried thyme

1/2 teaspoon (1 g) cayenne pepper

In small bowl, stir together marinade ingredients. Rub marinade over fillets. Place in glass or ceramic dish; cover and refrigerate for 20 to 30 minutes.

When ready to cook, heat large, heavy skillet over medium heat. Add oil and heat until shimmering. While oil is heating, dredge marinated fish in flour; add to hot oil and brown on both sides, 6 to 8 minutes total. Transfer fish to clean dish; set aside and keep warm.

Add onion and garlic to skillet; sauté until soft, 3 to 4 minutes. Add coconut milk, bay leaves, tamarind paste, paprika, thyme and cayenne pepper. Reduce heat and simmer mixture for 5 minutes, stirring occasionally. Return fish to skillet and cook until heated through, 2 to 3 minutes.

*Tamarind paste is a tart ingredient used in Thai cooking. Look for it in Asian specialty stores; you may also find it at a Latino market. If it looks stringy and has seeds, blend with a small amount of water, then strain out seeds and coarse material before using.

BAKED GROUPER WITH GARLIC, FENNEL AND SUN-DRIED TOMATOES

Serves 4
Preparation: Under 30 minutes

1¹/₂ pounds (680 g) skinless grouper fillets

1 whole head of garlic

Half of a head of fennel, cut into ¹/₄-inch (.6 cm) slices

¹/₂ cup (1.2 dl) dry white wine

¹/₂ cup (18.5 g) sun-dried tomatoes, sliced

3 tablespoons (45 ml) olive oil

Heat oven to 450°F (230°C). Place fillets, skinned side down, in shallow baking dish. Separate garlic cloves but do not peel. In mixing bowl, combine garlic cloves, fennel, wine, tomatoes and oil; stir well. Pour mixture over fish; bake for 8 to 10 minutes, or until just cooked through.

SALMON BAKED WITH MUSHROOMS AND HONEY MUSTARD

Serves 4
Preparation: Under 15 minutes

¹/₂ pound (225 g) mushrooms, thinly sliced

4 shallots, sliced

2 tablespoons (30 ml) olive oil, divided

1¹/₂ pounds (680 g) boneless, skinless salmon or steelhead fillet

2 tablespoons (30 g) honey mustard

Juice of 1 lemon

Heat oven to 450°F (230°C). Place mushrooms, shallots and 1 tablespoon (15 ml) of the oil into 9x13-inch (23x33 cm) baking dish. Place salmon on top. In small bowl, blend together remaining 1 tablespoon (15 ml) oil with the mustard and lemon juice. Spread mustard mixture over salmon. Bake for 8 to 10 minutes, or until desired doneness.

POACHED STEELHEAD WITH PORT AND BERRY SAUCE

Serves 4 to 6
Preparation: 30 to 60 minutes

1 quart (.95 l) fish stock (page 105), white wine or water

2 pounds (900 g) boneless, skinless steelhead or salmon fillet

¹/₂ cup (1.2 dl) port wine

4 shallots, minced

1 tablespoon (15 ml) balsamic vinegar

1 cup (120 g) raspberries, strawberries or cooked sugared cranberries

2 tablespoons (30 ml) cream

¹/₄ cup (55 g/half of a stick) butter, cut up

Select a pan large enough to hold steelhead in single layer. Add stock and heat to boiling over high heat. Gently lay steelhead into hot stock. As soon as stock returns to a boil, reduce heat so liquid is simmering; poach until just cooked through, 8 to 10 minutes. With long spatula, gently transfer steelhead to plate; set aside and keep warm. Discard all but 1 cup (2.3 dl) poaching liquid.

To stock remaining in pan, add port, shallots and vinegar. Boil over high heat until reduced by half. Add berries and cream and reduce by one-quarter. Turn off heat and add butter, a tablespoon at a time, stirring constantly. Pour sauce over steelhead and serve.

SEARED TUNA WITH PESTO

Serves 4
Preparation: Under 15 minutes

PESTO:

2 cups (75 g) fresh basil leaves, rinsed and dried

¹/₂ cup (70 g) toasted pine nuts (page 58), or toasted walnut or pecan halves

3 or 4 cloves garlic, peeled

¹/₂ cup (1.2 dl) olive oil

¹/₂ cup (63 g) grated Parmesan cheese

¹/₄ teaspoon (.5 g) pepper

¹/₂ teaspoon (3 g) salt

1 tablespoon (15 ml) olive oil

4 tuna steaks or other firm, meaty fish steaks, approximately ³/₄ inch (1.9 cm) thick (6 to 8 ounces/170 to 225 g each)

To make pesto: Place all pesto ingredients in food processor fitted with metal blade; process just until well mixed, 30 to 60 seconds. To cook tuna: Heat oil in large, heavy skillet over high heat. When oil is very hot, add tuna and sear for 3 to 4 minutes per side, or until desired doneness. Top with pesto and serve immediately.

Poached Steelhead with Port and Berry Sauce

FISH FILLETS BAKED IN PARCHMENT

Serves 4
Preparation: Under 15 minutes

This is an amazingly versatile method of cooking fish. Many different kinds of fish can be baked in parchment, and you can add any manner of seasoning or even other ingredients such as julienned vegetables, tomatoes or shellfish. It's perfect for entertaining, because the packets can be prepared in advance; actual cooking takes less than 10 minutes, and requires almost no attention from the cook.

4 sheets kitchen parchment paper, 16 inches (40.6 cm) long*

1½ pounds (680 g) halibut, rockfish or seabass fillets, divided into 4 equal portions

2 tablespoons (30 g) butter

2 tablespoons (5 to 10 g) minced fresh herbs such as dill, basil, tarragon or thyme

Juice and zest from 1 lemon

Heat oven to 450°F (230°C). For each serving, fold parchment paper in half; open again and place 1 portion of fish on bottom half, about 1 inch (2.5 cm) from crease. Top each fish portion with one-quarter of the butter and one-quarter of the herbs; sprinkle lemon juice and zest evenly over each portion. Enclose fish in parchment with a series of overlapping folds (see below). Place packets in single layer on baking sheet. Bake for 6 to 10 minutes, depending on thickness of fish; parchment paper will be puffed up and brown.

*IN A PINCH YOU CAN EVEN USE A LARGE, CLEAN PAPER BAG INSTEAD OF PARCHMENT PAPER.

HOW TO FOLD PARCHMENT

1. Fold parchment over seasoned fish (the folded edge is at the top).

2. Fold top left corner over toward fish.

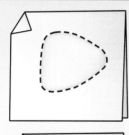

steps 1 and 2

3. Fold left edge over.

4. Fold bottom left edge and corner over, using several folds.

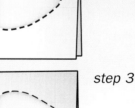

step 3

5. Fold bottom edge up.

6. Fold bottom right corner over toward fish.

7 and 8. Complete packet by folding right edge over until packet is sealed, using several folds.

steps 4 thru 8

COCONUT CURRIED SALMON MEDALLIONS

Serves 4 to 6
Preparation: Under 30 minutes

FLOUR MIXTURE:

½ cup (70 g) all-purpose flour

½ cup (53 g) finely chopped unsalted peanuts

1 tablespoon (6 g) curry powder

2 pounds (900 g) boneless, skinless salmon fillet, cut into 8 evenly sized pieces

¼ cup (60 ml) canola or other mild oil, divided

1 onion, diced

1 carrot, diced

2 teaspoons (4 g) curry powder

½ cup (1.2 dl) fish stock (page 105)

½ cup (1.2 dl) white wine

½ cup (83 g) raisins

½ cup (1.2 dl) coconut milk

In wide dish, stir together all flour-mixture ingredients. Dredge salmon in flour mixture. In large, heavy skillet, heat 2 tablespoons (30 ml) of the oil over medium heat until shimmering. Add salmon; cook for 2 to 3 minutes per side, until lightly browned and not quite cooked through. Transfer salmon to plate; set aside and keep warm.

Add remaining 2 tablespoons (30 ml) oil to skillet. Add onion and carrot; sauté until just soft, 3 to 4 minutes. Add curry powder, fish stock, wine and raisins; cook until reduced by half. Add coconut milk and salmon; simmer until salmon is cooked through, 2 to 3 minutes.

BAKED BLUEFISH WITH ORANGE AND GINGER

Serves 4
Preparation: Under 15 minutes

Bluefish is one of my favorite fishes, but it needs to be extremely fresh to taste its best. Mackerel also works great in this recipe, and both bluefish and mackerel are true bargains.

1/4 cup (60 ml) orange juice

2 tablespoons (30 ml) dark sesame oil

1 tablespoon (15 ml) lime juice

2 tablespoons (30 g) minced fresh gingerroot

2 tablespoons (5 g) chopped fresh cilantro

1 1/2 pounds (680 g) skin-on bluefish, mackerel, or other oily, full-flavored fish fillets

Heat oven to 450°F (230°C). In measuring cup or small bowl, stir together orange juice, sesame oil, lime juice, gingerroot and cilantro. Lay bluefish on baking sheet, skin side down; pour orange-juice mixture evenly over fish. Bake until just cooked through, 6 to 10 minutes, depending on thickness.

GRILLED MARINATED FISH STEAKS

Serves 4
Preparation: 30 to 60 minutes

1 1/4 cups (2.9 dl) olive oil

Juice from 2 lemons

1 tablespoon (15 g) minced garlic

1 tablespoon (15 g) coarse mustard

Pepper

1 1/2 pounds (680 g) cobia or swordfish steaks or substitute, approximately 3/4 inch (1.9 cm) thick

In small bowl, whisk together oil, lemon juice, garlic, mustard, and pepper to taste. Place steaks in single layer in baking dish. Pour marinade over steaks, turning to coat. Cover and refrigerate for 20 to 30 minutes; meanwhile, prepare charcoal or gas grill. Grill marinated steaks for 3 to 4 minutes per side, or until desired doneness.

SOLE FLORENTINE

Serves 4
Preparation: 30 to 60 minutes

2 tablespoons (30 g) minced garlic

1/4 cup (60 ml) olive oil, divided

1 pound (454 g) fresh, cleaned spinach

1/2 pound (225 g) ricotta cheese

3 tablespoons (27 g) toasted pine nuts

1 teaspoon (.75 g) dried thyme

1 teaspoon (.3 g) dried oregano

Salt and pepper

4 boneless, skinless sole fillets, 6 to 8 ounces (170 to 225 g) each

Heat oven to 450°F (230°C). In large, heavy skillet, sauté garlic in 2 tablespoons (30 ml) of the oil for about 2 minutes. Add spinach and cook until spinach wilts, 2 to 3 minutes longer. Remove from heat. Add ricotta, pine nuts, thyme, oregano, and salt and pepper to taste; mix gently but thoroughly. Place fillets on work surface and top with equal amounts of spinach mixture. Roll fillets around filling; arrange on baking sheet. Drizzle with remaining 2 tablespoons (30 ml) oil. Bake for 6 to 8 minutes, or until instant-read meat thermometer inserted into center of rolls registers 135°F to 140°F (57°C to 60°C).

BLACKENED TUNA

Serves 4 to 6
Preparation: Under 15 minutes

This recipe works perfectly with any oily, full-flavored fish such as bluefish, mackerel or marlin.

SEASONING BLEND:

1 teaspoon (6 g) salt

1/2 teaspoon (1.2 g) onion powder

1 teaspoon (2 g) paprika

1/4 teaspoon (.5 g) cayenne pepper

1/4 teaspoon (.5 g) black pepper

1/2 teaspoon (.2 g) dried oregano

1/2 teaspoon (.4 g) dried thyme

1/2 teaspoon (.2 g) dried basil

2 pounds (900 g) tuna steaks, approximately 3/4 inch (1.9 cm) thick

2 tablespoons (30 ml) canola or other mild oil

In small bowl, stir together all seasoning-blend ingredients. Sprinkle liberally over both sides of tuna steaks, pressing in gently with fingertips. Heat large cast-iron skillet over medium-high heat. When very hot, add oil and then seasoned tuna. Cook for 3 to 4 minutes on first side; flip over, reduce heat to low and continue cooking for 3 to 4 minutes longer, or until desired doneness.

SOLE FLORENTINE

MARLIN FAJITAS

MARLIN FAJITAS

Serves 4 to 6
Preparation: Under 15 minutes

3 tablespoons (45 ml) olive oil

2 pounds (900 g) marlin steaks or substitute, cut into strips approximately 1/2 inch (1.25 cm) thick

1 red bell pepper, cut into 1-inch (2.5 cm) chunks

1 green bell pepper, cut into 1-inch (2.5 cm) chunks

1 large onion, cut into 1-inch (2.5 cm) chunks

4 cloves garlic, minced

2 teaspoons (5 g) chili powder blend

1 teaspoon (2 g) cumin

1 teaspoon (2 g) hot paprika

Salt and pepper

1 package (16 ounces/454 g) burrito- or fajita-sized flour tortillas, warmed

Garnishes: Salsa, sour cream, guacamole

Heat large, heavy skillet on high heat. When hot, add oil and heat until shimmering. Add marlin; stir-fry for 3 to 4 minutes. Transfer marlin to plate. Add red and green bell peppers, onion and garlic to hot skillet and sauté until just barely soft, 3 to 4 minutes. Add marlin, chili powder, cumin, paprika, and salt and pepper to taste; sauté for 1 minute longer. Serve in flour tortillas with salsa, sour cream and guacamole.

FISH FILLETS BAKED WITH HERB BUTTER

Serves 4
Preparation: Under 15 minutes

Herb butters are a great way to preserve the flavor of fresh herbs. Whether you grow your own, or buy them at a farmers' market or grocery store, fresh herbs at the peak of their season are a great, convenient way to add flavor to fish. These herb butters freeze beautifully, either simply rolled up in wax paper or put in a tightly sealed plastic container.

3 tablespoons (45 g) butter, softened

3 tablespoons (8 to 16 g) minced fresh herbs (one or more of the following: dill, chervil, thyme, tarragon, basil, rosemary, marjoram*)

2 tablespoons (20 g) minced shallot

1 tablespoon (15 ml) lemon juice

1 1/2 to 2 pounds (680 to 900 g) mild flaky fish fillets, such as halibut, cod or haddock

Heat oven to 450°F (230°C). In small bowl, stir together butter, herbs, shallot and lemon juice. Arrange fish in an even layer on baking sheet; spread herb butter over fillets. Bake for 6 to 8 minutes, or until fish is cooked through.

*FEEL FREE TO SUBSTITUTE HERBS IN SEASON, OR YOUR FAVORITE HERB COMBINATIONS.

BAKED HALIBUT WITH SAFFRON CREAM SAUCE

Serves 4
Preparation: Under 30 minutes

1 1/2 pounds (680 g) halibut fillets

1/2 cup (1.2 dl) white wine

2 tablespoons (30 ml) canola or other mild oil

Salt and pepper

SAFFRON CREAM SAUCE:

4 shallots, minced

2 tablespoons (30 g) butter

1/2 cup (1.2 dl) white wine

2 teaspoons (.6 g) saffron threads

1 cup (2.3 dl) cream

Salt and white pepper

Heat oven to 450°F (230°C). Place halibut fillets in large baking dish. Pour wine and oil over fish; sprinkle with salt and pepper to taste. Bake for 8 to 10 minutes, or until just cooked through.

While halibut is baking, prepare sauce. In medium saucepan, sauté shallots in butter over medium heat until soft. Add wine and saffron; increase heat to high and boil until reduced to 1/4 cup (60 ml). Reduce heat to low and whisk in cream, and salt and white pepper to taste. When combined, increase heat to high and cook, stirring constantly, until reduced by one-half. Pour sauce over halibut and serve.

SAUTÉED SOLE WITH PECAN BUTTER

Serves 4
Preparation: Under 15 minutes

1/2 cup (60 g) coarsely chopped pecans

3 tablespoons (45 g) butter, softened

1 tablespoon (10 g) minced shallot

Juice and zest from 1 lemon

2 tablespoons (30 ml) canola oil

1 1/2 pounds (680 g) sole fillets

1/4 cup (35 g) all-purpose flour

In food processor fitted with metal blade, combine pecans, butter, shallot, lemon juice and zest; process until creamy and smooth, scraping sides with rubber spatula as necessary. Set aside.

Heat oil in large, heavy skillet over medium-high heat. When oil shimmers, dredge sole in flour and cook for 2 minutes. Turn sole, and cook on second side for 1 minute. Add pecan butter and cook for 1 minute longer.

HERB-MARINATED GRILLED BARRACUDA

Serves 4 to 6
Preparation: 30 to 60 minutes

Barracuda is a great-tasting fish, as well as one of the world's more popular sport fish. However, it is susceptible to ciguatera, a toxin picked up when fish feed on coral reefs. Ciguatera toxin is dangerous to humans, and care must be taken to ensure that the barracuda do not come from areas near reefs. Barracuda are extremely territorial, so responsibly harvested fish remain a safe treat. Their firm, sweet flesh reminds me greatly of pork tenderloin.

1/4 cup (60 ml) olive oil

1 tablespoon (15 ml) lemon juice

1 tablespoon (15 ml) orange juice

1 tablespoon (2 g) minced fresh rosemary

1 tablespoon (3 g) minced fresh basil

1 tablespoon (15 g) coarse mustard

1 teaspoon (6 g) salt

1/2 teaspoon (1 g) pepper

2 bay leaves, crushed

2 pounds (900 g) barracuda fillets

In small bowl, combine all ingredients except barracuda; mix well. Place fillets in single layer in baking dish. Pour marinade over fillets, turning to coat. Cover and refrigerate for 20 to 30 minutes; meanwhile, prepare charcoal or gas grill. Put fillets, flesh side down, on grate. After about 5 minutes, flip over and continue grilling until barracuda is just cooked through and opaque.

SAUTÉED STURGEON WITH WINE AND MUSHROOMS

Serves 4 to 6
Preparation: Under 30 minutes

1/4 cup (60 ml) olive oil

3 tablespoons (22 g) all-purpose flour

1 teaspoon (6 g) salt

1/2 teaspoon (1 g) pepper

2 pounds (900 g) skinless sturgeon fillet, cut into 1/2-inch-thick (1.25 cm) "steaks"

1/2 pound (225 g) mushrooms, sliced

3 shallots, minced

1/2 cup (1.2 dl) white wine

1 tablespoon (15 ml) lemon juice

Add oil to large, heavy skillet and begin heating over medium-high heat. Meanwhile, in shallow bowl, stir together flour, salt and pepper. When oil is very hot but not quite smoking, dredge sturgeon with seasoned flour; cook for 2 minutes per side, until browned. Remove fish from skillet; set aside and keep warm. Add mushrooms and shallots to hot skillet. Sauté for 2 to 3 minutes. Add wine and lemon juice; continue cooking until sauce is reduced by one-half. Return sturgeon to pan and braise for about 1 minute per side, or until cooked through.

STRIPED BASS BAKED WITH FENNEL, GARLIC AND TOMATO

Serves 4 to 6
Preparation: Under 15 minutes

2 pounds (900 g) skin-on, scaled striped bass fillets,* approximately 1¼ inches (3.2 cm) thick

1 head of fennel, diced

1 onion, diced

Half of a head of garlic, peeled and roughly chopped

1 cup (180 g) diced tomatoes

3 bay leaves

1 cup (2.3 dl) white wine

1/4 cup (60 ml) olive oil

1 teaspoon (.75 g) dried thyme

1 teaspoon (6 g) salt

1/2 teaspoon (1 g) pepper

Heat oven to 450°F (230°C). Place fillets, skin side down, in large baking dish. Scatter fennel, onion, garlic, tomatoes and bay leaves on top of and around fillets. Pour wine and oil over fillets; sprinkle with thyme, salt and pepper. Bake for 12 to 15 minutes or until cooked through, basting with pan juices every 5 minutes or so.

*YOU MAY USE SKINLESS FILLETS IF YOU PREFER.

SKATE WITH BLACK BUTTER AND CAPERS

Serves 4
Preparation: Under 30 minutes

Skate, or ray, is one of my favorite "underutilized" species. Much of the world's skate is caught in the Eastern United States and in the Pacific Northwest. Most of this catch finds its way to Europe and Asia, where it is considered one of the finest fish available. Skate is so commonly eaten in France that at times it has been part of the French school lunch program. In the United States, consumers' lack of familiarity with skate has caused it to be one of the true bargains in the seafood business. Skate has a very short shelf life, however, and should be consumed within a day or two of purchase.

3 cups (6.9 dl) fish stock (page 105)

1 cup (2.3 dl) white wine

1 tablespoon (15 ml) apple cider vinegar

1 teaspoon (2 g) whole black peppercorns

2 bay leaves

2 pounds (900 g) skinless skate wing, or 1¹/₂ pounds (680 g) skate fillets

¹/₂ cup (110 g/1 stick) butter

2 tablespoons (20 g) drained capers

Juice of 1 lemon

Salt and pepper

In large pot, combine fish stock, wine, vinegar, peppercorns and bay leaves. Heat to boiling over high heat. Carefully lower skate into stock and reduce heat to low. Poach skate for 6 to 10 minutes, depending on thickness. While skate is poaching, in small skillet or saucepan, cook butter over medium-low heat until it is medium brown and smells nutty. Add capers, lemon juice, and salt and pepper to taste; remove from heat. When skate is just cooked through, carefully lift out of stock and transfer to serving plate; pour caper butter on top.

SESAME SAUTÉED WAHOO

Serves 4 to 6
Preparation: Under 15 minutes

Wahoo, also called ono, is a larger—and delicious—member of the mackerel family. It is firm and sweet with a moderate oil content, and is very similar to swordfish and shark in cooking characteristics.

1/4 cup (40 g) white sesame seeds

2 pounds (900 g) wahoo steaks, approximately 3/4 inch (1.9 cm) thick

3 tablespoons (45 ml) canola or other mild oil

2 tablespoons (30 g) minced fresh gingerroot

1 tablespoon (15 g) minced garlic

2 tablespoons (30 ml) lime juice

2 tablespoons (30 ml) dark sesame oil

2 tablespoons (30 ml) soy sauce

Press sesame seeds firmly onto both sides of wahoo steaks; some will fall off, and this is fine. Heat large, heavy skillet over medium-high heat. Add oil and heat until shimmering. Sear wahoo steaks for 2 minutes per side. Add gingerroot, garlic, lime juice, sesame oil and soy sauce to skillet; braise for an additional 1 to 2 minutes per side, or until wahoo is cooked through.

ITALIAN SAUTÉED TAUTOG OR SEABASS

Serves 4 to 6
Preparation: Under 30 minutes

Tautog is a delicious fish that is a member of the wrasse family. Found primarily from Canada south to the Carolinas, they have firm, white flesh that is extremely sweet. Most tautog are caught by sport anglers, although some are sold commercially; they are usually referred to as blackfish when sold commercially.

1/2 cup (70 g) all-purpose flour

1 teaspoon (6 g) salt

1/2 teaspoon (1 g) pepper

1/4 cup plus 1 tablespoon (75 ml) olive oil

2 pounds (900 g) boneless, skinless tautog or seabass fillets

1 cup (2.3 dl) white wine

1/2 cup (70 g) pitted green olives

1 tablespoon (10 g) drained capers

1/2 teaspoon (.2 g) dried basil

1/2 teaspoon (.2 g) dried oregano

3 cloves garlic, chopped

In shallow dish, combine flour, salt and pepper. In large, heavy skillet, heat oil over medium-high heat. When oil is very hot but not quite smoking, dredge fillets in seasoned flour and place in skillet, skinned side up. Cook for 3 to 4 minutes, or until brown. Turn and cook for 3 minutes on second side. Carefully transfer fillets to plate; set aside and keep warm.

Add wine, olives, capers, basil, oregano and garlic to hot skillet, scraping bottom of skillet to loosen browned bits. Boil until reduced by two-thirds. Return fillets to skillet, then turn over gently to coat with sauce. Serve fillets with sauce on top.

CRISPY MUSTARD-BAKED MACKEREL

Serves 4
Preparation: Under 30 minutes

1/4 cup (28 g) breadcrumbs

2 tablespoons (8 g) minced flat-leaf (Italian) parsley

1 tablespoon (15 g) mayonnaise

1 tablespoon (15 g) coarse mustard

1 tablespoon (15 ml) lemon juice

Salt and pepper

1 1/2 pounds (680 g) mackerel, bluefish or other oily, full-flavored fish fillets

2 tablespoons (30 ml) olive oil

Heat oven to 450°F (230°C). In small bowl, combine breadcrumbs, parsley, mayonnaise, mustard, lemon juice, and salt and pepper to taste; stir gently to combine. Arrange mackerel fillets on baking sheet or large baking dish; top with mustard crumbs. Drizzle evenly with oil. Bake for 8 to 10 minutes, or until cooked through.

BASIC PAN-FRIED FISH

Serves 4
Preparation: Under 15 minutes

This recipe works great for any fish that takes well to frying. For variety, try mixing ground nuts with the flour, or dried seasoning with the crumbs.

1 egg

1/2 cup (1.2 dl) milk

1/2 cup (70 g) all-purpose flour

Salt and pepper

1/2 cup (80 g) cornmeal, cracker crumbs or breadcrumbs

1/4 cup (60 ml) canola or other mild oil

1 1/2 pounds (680 g) boneless, skinless lean, flaky fish fillets such as cod, haddock or halibut

Lightly beat egg and milk together in small bowl. Pour flour into separate bowl; season to taste with salt and pepper. Place cornmeal into third bowl. Heat oil in large, heavy skillet over medium heat. Dredge fish first in flour, then egg wash, and finally in cornmeal. When oil is hot, add fish fillets and fry for 3 to 4 minutes per side, or until golden brown and cooked through.

SAUTÉED WEAKFISH WITH BACON, MUSHROOMS AND ONION

Serves 4 to 6
Preparation: Under 30 minutes

Weakfish, also called sea trout, are found from Maine down south to the Carolinas. They have moderately oily flesh and a delicious sweet, nutty flavor. The name weakfish comes from their soft, weak mouths, which tend to rip easily when hooked.

3 tablespoons (45 ml) canola or other mild oil

2 pounds (900 g) skin-on, scaled weakfish fillets

1/2 cup (70 g) all-purpose flour

1/4 pound (113 g) sliced bacon, cut into 1/4-inch (.6 cm) pieces

1 large onion, diced

1/2 pound (225 g) mushrooms, quartered

2 tablespoons (30 ml) lemon juice

1 tablespoon (2 g) minced fresh rosemary

1 teaspoon (6 g) salt

1/2 teaspoon (1 g) pepper

In large, heavy skillet, heat oil over medium-high heat. When oil is very hot but not quite smoking, dredge fillets in flour and place in skillet, skinned side up. Cook for 3 minutes per side, or until brown. Carefully transfer fillets to plate; set aside and keep warm.

Reduce heat to medium; add bacon and sauté for 3 minutes. Add onion and mushrooms; sauté for 3 to 4 minutes longer. Add lemon juice, rosemary, salt and pepper. Return browned fillets to pan; reheat fillets for a minute or so. Serve with bacon mixture on top.

BAKED LINGCOD WITH APPLES AND MINT SAUCE

Serves 4 to 6
Preparation: Under 30 minutes

Lingcod, despite its name, is not a member of the cod family but rather a greenling. These fish can be caught anywhere from Southern California up through Alaska, and are a highly revered species on the Pacific Coast. The flesh of lingcod is moderately lean and has a sweet, mild flavor.

2 pounds (900 g) boneless, skinless lingcod fillet(s), approximately 3/4 inch (1.9 cm) thick

1/2 cup (1.2 dl) white wine

2 tart apples, peeled, cored and cut into thick slices

MINT SAUCE:

1/2 cup (30 g) fresh mint leaves

1/2 cup (30 g) flat-leaf (Italian) parsley

1/4 cup (53 g) chopped walnuts

2 shallots, minced

1/2 cup (1.2 dl) olive oil

1 teaspoon (6 g) salt

1/4 teaspoon (.5 g) pepper

Heat oven to 450°F (230°C). Place fillets in large baking dish. Pour wine over fish; arrange apple slices around edges. In food processor fitted with metal blade, combine all mint-sauce ingredients; process until smooth. With rubber spatula, spread mint sauce over and around the fillets. Bake for approximately 8 minutes, or until just cooked through.

SAUTÉED COBIA WITH FRESH HERB AND WALNUT SAUCE

Serves 4 to 6
Preparation: 30 to 60 minutes

1 cup (40 g) fresh basil leaves

1/2 cup (30 g) walnut halves

3 cloves garlic, roughly chopped

1/2 cup plus 3 tablespoons (1.65 dl) olive oil, divided

2 pounds (900 g) cobia or snook, cut into 3/4-inch-thick (1.9 cm) steaks

In food processor fitted with metal blade, combine basil, walnuts, garlic and 1/2 cup (1.2 dl) of the oil; process until smooth. Heat remaining 3 tablespoons (45 ml) of the oil in large, heavy skillet over medium-high heat. When oil is very hot but not quite smoking, add fish steaks and sear for 3 minutes per side. Add basil purée to skillet; cook for 1 minute longer. Serve fish with basil sauce on top.

SEARED SHARK WITH TOMATO SALSA

Serves 4
Preparation: Under 30 minutes

SALSA:

1 jalapeño or other hot pepper

6 roma tomatoes, finely diced

3 cloves garlic, minced

Half of a bunch of cilantro, chopped

1 tablespoon (15 ml) lemon juice

1 tablespoon (15 ml) lime juice

3 tablespoons (45 ml) olive oil

1½ pounds (680 g) skinless, boneless shark or swordfish steak, cut into 1-inch (2.5 cm) cubes

Cut jalapeño in half lengthwise; discard seeds and stem. Mince jalapeño finely; combine in mixing bowl with remaining salsa ingredients. Set aside.

Heat large, heavy skillet over high heat. Add oil and heat until it just begins to smoke. Add shark cubes to skillet; stir-fry for 5 to 6 minutes, or until shark is almost cooked through. Pour salsa into pan, toss very quickly with shark and serve.

SALMON STEAMED IN NAPA CABBAGE

SALMON STEAMED IN NAPA CABBAGE

THE SALTWATER COOKBOOK

SALMON STEAMED IN NAPA CABBAGE

Serves 6
Preparation: Under 30 minutes

12 large napa cabbage leaves

1½ pounds (680 g) boneless salmon fillet, cut into 6 serving-sized portions

⅓ cup (20 g) chopped fresh tarragon, basil, or thyme

2 cups (4.6 dl) white wine or fish stock

1 cup (2.3 dl) cream

2 tablespoons (30 g) Dijon mustard

Blanch cabbage leaves for about a minute in large pot of boiling water; drain, refresh with cold water, and pat dry. Lay 2 cabbage leaves, side by side and slightly overlapping, on work surface. Place portion of salmon in center; top with herbs. Fold leaves closed over salmon. Arrange wrapped salmon bundles on steamer rack in single layer. Heat wine to boiling in bottom of steamer. Add rack, cover tightly, and steam for 8 to 10 minutes, or until salmon is almost cooked through. Transfer salmon bundles to plate; set aside and keep warm. Add cream to wine and cook over high heat until reduced by half. Stir in mustard and serve over salmon.

PASTA WITH ROSEMARY, GREEN APPLES AND SMOKED FISH

Serves 4 to 6
Preparation: 30 to 60 minutes

This is a delightful, rich pasta dish that is great served with a simple green salad. You can easily substitute any other smoked fish for the cold-smoked salmon. I have used smoked rainbow trout very successfully in this recipe.

1 cup (2.3 dl) dry white wine

4 shallots, minced

2 tablespoons (3 g) whole fresh rosemary leaves

1 tart apple, peeled, cored and diced

1 cup (2.3 dl) cream

2 tablespoons (30 ml) brandy

2 tablespoons (30 g) butter

½ cup grated (63 g) Parmesan cheese

½ pound (225 g) finely sliced cold-smoked salmon

1 pound (454 g) packaged fettuccine

Begin heating large pot of salted water for cooking pasta. In medium saucepan, combine wine, shallots and rosemary. Heat to boiling and cook until reduced by three-quarters. During this time, cook fettuccine according to package directions. Add apple and cream to wine mixture; continue cooking until reduced by half. Remove from heat; add brandy, butter, Parmesan cheese and salmon, stirring gently to mix well. Toss with hot cooked pasta.

SHERMOULA

Serves 6 to 8
Preparation: 1 to 2 hours marinating, plus about 45 minutes cooking time

This sweet, spicy dish is one of my favorite recipes for entertaining, as the entire dish can be made a day ahead of time. I prefer serving this at room temperature, although it is equally good served hot or cold. It's lovely presented around a mound of couscous.

2 pounds (900 g) boneless, skinless seabass or grouper fillets

2 tablespoons (30 g) harissa paste,* divided

1 teaspoon (2 g) ground cumin

1 teaspoon (2 g) cinnamon

¼ cup (60 ml) olive oil, divided

½ cup (70 g) all-purpose flour

2 large onions, julienned

¼ cup (40 g) raisins

¼ cup (60 ml) apple cider vinegar

¼ cup (60 ml) water

¼ cup (60 ml) honey

1 teaspoon curry powder or paste (5 g paste, 2 g powder)

Dice fish into approximately 1-inch (2.5 cm) cubes. In mixing bowl, stir together 1 tablespoon (15 g) of the harissa, the cumin and cinnamon. Add fish; stir gently to coat. Cover and refrigerate for 1 to 2 hours.

Heat large, heavy skillet over medium-high heat. Add 2 tablespoons (30 ml) of the oil and heat until hot but not smoking. While oil is heating, dredge marinated fish in flour; add to hot oil and brown on both sides, 4 to 5 minutes total. Transfer fish to dish; set aside and keep warm.

Add remaining 2 tablespoons (30 ml) of the oil and the onions to skillet. Reduce heat to low and cook, stirring occasionally, until onions are very soft and caramelized, 10 to 15 minutes. Add remaining 1 tablespoon (15 g) of the harissa, and the raisins, vinegar, water, honey and curry powder. Reduce heat to low and simmer for 5 to 10 minutes. Add fish and cook until warmed through, 1 to 2 minutes.

*HARISSA IS AN INCENDIARY PASTE OF CHILES, GARLIC, OIL AND SPICES THAT ORIGINATED IN NORTH AFRICA AND THE MIDDLE EAST. THERE'S A RECIPE FOR HARISSA ON PAGE 90; YOU CAN ALSO FIND IT IN SPECIALTY GROCERY STORES. THERE IS NO SUBSTITUTE.

INDIAN DRY CURRIED SHRIMP

Serves 4
Preparation: Under 15 minutes

1 onion, julienned

2 tablespoons (30 ml) peanut or dark sesame oil

3 cloves garlic, minced

1 teaspoon (2 g) ground coriander

1/2 teaspoon (1 g) turmeric

1/2 teaspoon (1 g) ground cumin

1/2 teaspoon (3 g) salt

1/4 teaspoon (.5 g) ground ginger

1/4 teaspoon (.5 g) black pepper

1/4 teaspoon (.6 g) chili powder blend

1 pound (454 g) peeled and deveined raw shrimp

1 tablespoon (15 ml) rice vinegar

In large, heavy skillet, sauté onion in oil over medium heat until almost soft. Add garlic and sauté for 1 to 2 minutes longer. Add coriander, turmeric, cumin, salt, ginger, black pepper and chili powder; cook for 1 to 2 minutes, stirring constantly. Add shrimp; sauté for 3 to 4 minutes, until almost cooked through. Stir in vinegar, cook for 1 minute longer, and serve immediately.

ROCK SHRIMP WITH CASHEWS AND BOURBON

Serves 4
Preparation: Under 15 minutes

2 tablespoons (30 ml) peanut or light sesame oil

1 pound (454 g) peeled and deveined raw rock shrimp or other shrimp

1/2 cup (80 g) unsalted cashew halves, chopped

4 shallots, chopped

1/2 cup (1.2 dl) bourbon

2 tablespoons (30 g) butter

Heat large, heavy skillet over high heat. Add oil and heat until oil just begins to smoke. Add shrimp, cashews and shallots. Sauté for 3 minutes, then scrape mixture into medium bowl and set aside. Place empty skillet over low heat. Carefully add bourbon, stepping away immediately to avoid the flames that will ignite from the bourbon. When flames subside, remove from heat; add butter and shrimp mixture to skillet. Toss shrimp with sauce and serve immediately.

SHRIMP, MANGO AND POTATO CURRY

Serves 4 to 6
Preparation: 30 to 60 minutes

This recipe would work equally well using scallops—or even a firm-fleshed fish such as marlin or swordfish, cut into chunks—in place of the shrimp. Serve over rice or noodles.

1 onion, diced

Half of a head of garlic, peeled and minced

2 tablespoons (30 g) minced fresh gingerroot

3 tablespoons (45 g) butter

2 cups (4.6 dl) fish stock (page 105), white wine or water

1/2 cup (90 g) diced tomatoes

2 tablespoons curry paste or powder (30 g paste, 12 g powder)

2 large potatoes, peeled and diced into approximately 1/2-inch (1.25 cm) cubes

11/2 pounds (680 g) peeled and deveined raw shrimp

1 mango, peeled and diced

In large, heavy skillet, sauté onion, garlic and gingerroot in butter over medium-low heat until soft. Add stock, tomatoes, curry paste and potatoes; simmer until potatoes are just barely tender, 15 to 20 minutes, stirring occasionally. Add shrimp and mango; continue simmering until shrimp is just cooked through, 4 to 5 minutes.

CAJUN BARBECUED SHRIMP

Serves 4 to 6
Preparation: Under 15 minutes

This classic Cajun dish is typically prepared with whole, heads-on shrimp that have not been deveined. Traditionally, diners pinch the heads off the cooked shrimp and suck the delicious fat from the inside of the head before eating the tail. If this is a bit too "authentic" for you, feel free to substitute headless, shell-on shrimp instead. The shells protect the shrimp from overcooking, and also add much flavor to the dish.

SPICE MIXTURE:

1 teaspoon (.75 g) dried thyme

1 teaspoon (.3 g) dried basil

1 teaspoon (.3 g) dried oregano

1 teaspoon (.75 g) dried marjoram

1 teaspoon (2.5 g) onion powder

1/2 teaspoon (1 g) cayenne pepper

1/2 teaspoon (1 g) black pepper

1/4 cup plus 1 tablespoon (75 ml) olive oil

1 1/2 pounds (680 g) whole, shell-on raw shrimp

2 tablespoons (30 g) minced garlic

1 tablespoon (15 g) tomato paste

Juice from 1 lemon

3 tablespoons (45 g) butter

In small bowl, stir together all spice-mixture ingredients; set aside. In large, heavy skillet, heat oil over high heat. When oil is very hot but not quite smoking, add shrimp; sauté for 2 to 3 minutes. Add garlic; sauté for another minute. Add spice mixture and continue cooking for about 1 minute longer. Add tomato paste, lemon juice and butter. Cook for about 1 minute longer; serve immediately.

CURRIED STUFFED LOBSTER ON THE GRILL

CURRIED STUFFED LOBSTER ON THE GRILL

Serves 2
Preparation: 30 to 60 minutes

To prevent the lobster from curling, you may want to slide a bamboo or metal skewer down the back of the lobster from the tail to the head before cooking.

2 live lobsters, 1 to 1¹/₂ pounds (454 to 600 g) each

¹/₄ cup (45 g) diced red onion

¹/₄ cup (37 g) diced red bell pepper

¹/₄ cup (37 g) diced green bell pepper

¹/₄ cup (25 g) chopped green onions (white and green parts)

¹/₄ cup (26 g) chopped walnuts

1 firm, tart apple, peeled, cored and diced

2 tablespoons (30 g) minced garlic

3 tablespoons (45 ml) peanut or light sesame oil

2 tablespoons (30 ml) dry sherry

1 tablespoon curry paste or powder (15 g paste, 6 g powder)

Prepare charcoal or gas grill. Kill lobsters by placing them on cutting board, then quickly piercing the back of the head with a knife. Butterfly lobsters by cutting underside from head to tail, then opening out flat. Crack claws with back of heavy knife. Remove and discard stomach sac, tomalley and intestinal tract.

Prepare stuffing: In large, heavy skillet, sauté red onion, red and green bell peppers, green onions, walnuts, apple and garlic in oil over medium heat for 4 to 5 minutes. Add sherry and curry paste; cook for about 1 minute longer. Gently spoon stuffing mixture into split sides of lobsters. Place lobsters on hot grill, shell side down; cover grill. Cook for 8 to 12 minutes, depending on size of lobster (don't flip lobsters over). When done, lobster meat should be opaque and will separate easy from shell.

NOTE: THIS RECIPE COULD ALSO BE PREPARED IN A 450°F (230°C) OVEN. JUST LAY THE STUFFED LOBSTERS ON A BAKING SHEET, THEN BAKE AS DIRECTED.

HOW TO KILL A LOBSTER

1. Keep the rubber band around each claw.

2. With one hand, grasp the lobster's tail where it joins the body. Hold a 10-inch chef's knife in the other hand, keeping the blade facing away from the hand holding the tail.

3. Place the point of the knife about 1 to 1¹/₂ inches from between the eyes toward the tail. Press quickly into the head through to the cutting board. Bring the blade down between the eyes to finish the cut of the head.

CARIBBEAN OKRA AND SHRIMP

Serves 4 to 6
Preparation: About 1 hour

1¹/₂ pounds (680 g) peeled and deveined raw shrimp

4 cloves garlic, minced

Juice and zest from 1 lemon

2 tablespoons (30 ml) peanut or light sesame oil

1 onion, diced

1 pound (454 g) okra, sliced into ¹/₂-inch (1.25 cm) pieces

¹/₂ cup (90 g) diced tomatoes

2 tablespoons (5 g) chopped fresh cilantro

1 teaspoon (2 g) ground cumin

¹/₂ teaspoon (1 g) allspice

¹/₂ teaspoon (1 g) cinnamon

¹/₂ teaspoon (1 g) cayenne pepper

Salt and black pepper

Hot cooked rice

In nonreactive bowl, combine shrimp with garlic, lemon juice and zest, stirring to coat. Cover and refrigerate for 20 to 30 minutes. In large, heavy skillet, heat oil over high heat until shimmering. Add shrimp mixture; sear for 1 to 2 minutes, stirring frequently. Use slotted spoon to transfer shrimp to clean dish; set aside and keep warm.

In same skillet, sauté onion over medium heat until soft and translucent. Add okra, tomatoes, cilantro, cumin, allspice, cinnamon, cayenne pepper, and salt and black pepper to taste; simmer until okra is just barely soft, 10 to 15 minutes, stirring occasionally. Return shrimp to skillet and cook for 2 minutes longer. Serve over rice.

LOBSTER RISOTTO

Serves 6 to 8
Preparation: Over 1 hour

Arborio rice is a short-grained, glutinous rice commonly used in risotto. Look for it at larger supermarkets, or at specialty Italian stores.

3 cups (6.9 dl) fish stock (page 105)

2 cups (4.6 dl) chicken broth

1 cup (2.3 dl) dry white wine

2 live lobsters, 1 to 1½ pounds (454 to 680 g) each

1 pound (454 g) mushrooms, quartered

1 onion, diced

1 green bell pepper, diced

3 shallots, minced

¼ cup (60 ml) olive oil

1 pound (454 g) uncooked arborio rice (about 2 cups)

1 cup (125 g) grated Parmesan cheese

2 tablespoons (5 g) minced fresh basil, or 1 tablespoon (1 g) dried

2 tablespoons (6 g) minced fresh tarragon, or 1 tablespoon (1 g) dried

In large pot, combine fish stock, chicken broth and wine; heat to boiling over high heat. Add lobsters and boil for 8 to 10 minutes. Remove lobsters from pot and set aside until cool enough to handle. Remove lobster meat from shells; return shells to pot. Chop meat into large pieces and set aside. Simmer shells in stock mixture for 30 minutes; strain stock, discarding shells. Keep stock simmering while cooking risotto.

In large, heavy pot or small stockpot, sauté mushrooms, onion, pepper and shallots in oil over medium heat until just barely soft. Add rice; sauté for 3 to 4 minutes longer. Reduce heat to low and add 1 cup (2.3 dl) of the simmering stock. Cook, stirring constantly, until stock is absorbed. Continue in this manner, adding stock in 1-cup (2.3 dl) portions and stirring until stock is absorbed, until rice is just cooked through; total cooking time will be 20 to 25 minutes. Rice should be *al dente*: firm to the bite but not crunchy. When rice is cooked, stir in lobster meat, Parmesan cheese, basil and tarragon; add a bit more stock if necessary to make the mixture creamy. Serve immediately.

SHRIMP CREOLE

Serves 6
Preparation: 30 to 60 minutes

1 onion, diced

1 red bell pepper, diced

4 ribs celery, diced

Half of a head of garlic, peeled and minced

¼ cup (60 ml) olive oil

2 cups (360 g) diced tomatoes

1 cup (2.3 dl) dry white wine

Juice from 1 lemon

2 bay leaves

1 teaspoon (2 g) black pepper

1 tablespoon (2.5 g) dried thyme

1 tablespoon (1 g) dried basil

1 teaspoon (2 g) paprika

½ teaspoon (1 g) cayenne pepper

½ teaspoon (1.5 g) dry mustard powder

2 pounds (900 g) peeled and deveined raw shrimp

Hot cooked rice

In large, heavy skillet, sauté onion, pepper, celery and garlic in oil over medium-high heat until barely soft. Add tomatoes, wine, lemon juice, bay leaves, black pepper, thyme, basil, paprika, cayenne and dry mustard. Heat to boiling; cook until reduced by one-third, 5 to 10 minutes. Add shrimp; reduce heat and simmer until shrimp is cooked through, 4 to 5 minutes. Serve over rice.

LOUISIANA SHRIMP SAUCE

Serves 4 to 6
Preparation: 30 to 60 minutes

1½ pounds (680 g) shell-on raw shrimp

1 carrot, diced

1 onion, diced

1 rib celery, diced

6 cloves garlic, roughly chopped

1 small hot pepper, seeded and roughly chopped

1 teaspoon (.3 g) dried basil

1 teaspoon (.75 g) dried thyme

1 teaspoon (.75 g) dried marjoram

¼ cup plus 2 tablespoons (90 ml) olive oil, divided

1 cup (2.3 dl) white wine

1 cup (2.3 dl) fish stock (page 105)

1 cup (180 g) diced tomatoes

Juice from 1 lemon

½ teaspoon (3 g) salt

¼ teaspoon (.5 g) pepper

Peel and devein shrimp, reserving shells. In large skillet, sauté shrimp shells, carrot, onion, celery, garlic, hot pepper, basil, thyme and marjoram in ¼ cup (60 ml) of the oil over medium heat for 5 minutes. Add wine, fish stock and tomatoes; adjust heat and simmer for 30 minutes. Strain sauce, discarding solids.

Return sauce to skillet and cook over medium-high heat until reduced by one-third. In separate large skillet, sauté shrimp in remaining 2 tablespoons (30 ml) of the oil over high heat for 2 minutes. Add lemon juice, salt and pepper; pour sauce over shrimp. Simmer for 1 minute longer and serve over rice or pasta.

SAUTÉED SOFT-SHELL CRAB

Serves 4
Preparation: Under 15 minutes

From early May through September, East Coast blue crabs start to molt. Once they lose their shell, they become one of the world's greatest culinary treasures—until they begin to grow a new shell, approximately 24 hours later. Soft-shelled crabs are sold by size, with the largest called whales, followed by jumbo, prime and hotels.

½ cup (70 g) all-purpose flour

1 teaspoon (2 g) paprika

1 teaspoon (6 g) salt

½ teaspoon (1 g) pepper

8 dressed "hotel-sized" soft-shell crabs,* or 4
   "jumbo-" or "whale-sized"*

2 tablespoons (30 ml) canola or other mild oil

2 tablespoons (30 g) butter

Juice of 1 lemon

In bowl, mix flour, paprika, salt and pepper; dredge crabs lightly. In large skillet, heat oil and butter over medium-high heat until just barely smoking. Add crabs; cook for about 2 minutes per side, until golden brown and just cooked through. Sprinkle lemon juice over crabs in skillet and serve at once.

*IF YOU BUY SOFT-SHELLED CRABS LIVE, IT IS VERY EASY TO DRESS THEM. SIMPLY REMOVE THE CRAB'S APRON, GILLS AND FACE AND YOU ARE READY TO GO (SEE PAGE 31 FOR DETAILS).

Portuguese Steamed Clams

PORTUGUESE STEAMED CLAMS

Serves 4 to 6
Preparation: Under 15 minutes

This recipe can be served over rice or pasta for a great and spicy 10-minute meal.

2 tablespoons (30 ml) olive oil

1/2 pound (225 g) chorizo or other spicy sausage, crumbled (casings removed if links)

1 onion, diced

Half of a head of garlic, peeled and chopped

2 bay leaves

1 tablespoon (2.5 g) dried thyme

1 teaspoon (.3 g) dried oregano

1 teaspoon (2 g) hot paprika

1 cup (180 g) diced tomatoes

1 cup (2.3 dl) white wine or fish stock (page 105)

2 pounds (900 g) scrubbed clams

In large, heavy skillet that has a tight-fitting lid, heat oil over medium heat until warm. Add chorizo, onion, garlic, bay leaves, thyme, oregano and paprika; sauté for 4 to 6 minutes, or until chorizo is lightly browned. Add tomatoes and wine; heat to boiling. Add clams. Cover skillet tightly and steam until clams open, about 5 minutes; discard any clams that don't open.

GREEK SHRIMP WITH FETA AND OLIVES

Serves 4 to 6
Preparation: Under 30 minutes

This is delicious served over rice or orzo, a Greek pasta that is similar in size to rice.

1 onion, diced

6 cloves garlic, minced

1/4 cup (60 ml) olive oil

2 cups (360 g) diced tomatoes

1/2 cup (1.2 dl) dry white wine

2 tablespoons (30 g) tomato paste

1 tablespoon (1 g) dried oregano

1 tablespoon (1 g) dried basil

1 tablespoon (3 g) snipped fresh dill weed

1 1/2 pounds (680 g) peeled and deveined raw shrimp

8 ounces (225 g) crumbled feta cheese

1/2 cup (70 g) pitted kalamata olives

In large skillet, sauté onion and garlic in oil over medium heat until soft. Add tomatoes, wine, tomato paste, oregano, basil and dill. Reduce heat to low and simmer for 10 minutes. Increase heat to high. Add shrimp; sauté until just cooked through, 3 to 4 minutes. Remove from heat; stir in feta and olives, and serve immediately.

MUSSELS AND FETTUCCINE

Serves 4 to 6
Preparation: 30 to 60 minutes

Feel free to substitute clams for the mussels, or use a combination of the two.

1 cup (2.3 dl) fish stock (page 105)

1 cup (2.3 dl) white wine

1 cup (120 g) diced fennel

4 cloves garlic, chopped

2 pounds (900 g) fresh, live mussels, scrubbed, beards removed (page 28)

1 pound (454 g) packaged fettuccine

2 tablespoons chopped fresh basil (5 g) or rosemary (3 g)

1/4 cup (55 g/half of a stick) butter

Grated Parmesan cheese for serving, optional

Begin heating large pot of salted water to boiling for cooking pasta. In large, heavy skillet that has a tight-fitting lid, combine fish stock, wine, fennel and garlic; heat to boiling over high heat. Add mussels. Cover tightly and steam just until mussels open. Check your pan every couple of minutes and remove mussels as they open, transferring to a dish and keeping warm. Discard any mussels that haven't opened after about 5 minutes.

Boil stock mixture, uncovered, until liquid has reduced by three-quarters; during this time, cook fettuccine according to package directions. When stock mixture has reduced, add basil; cook for about 1 minute longer. Remove from heat and whisk in butter, a tablespoon (15 g) at a time. Add mussels; drain cooked fettuccine and toss with mussels and sauce. Serve with Parmesan cheese.

SAUTÉED SCALLOPS WITH MUSTARD AND CREAM

Serves 4 to 6
Preparation: 15 to 30 minutes

3 tablespoons (45 ml) canola or other mild oil

1½ pounds (680 g) sea or bay scallops

½ cup (70 g) all-purpose flour

½ cup (1.2 dl) white wine

½ cup (1.2 dl) cream

2 tablespoons (30 g) Dijon mustard

Salt and white pepper

In large, heavy skillet, heat oil over high heat. Meanwhile, dredge scallops with flour and lay on clean, dry plate. When oil is very hot, add scallops and cook, stirring constantly, for 4 to 6 minutes, depending on size of scallops. Transfer scallops to dish; set aside and keep warm. Add wine to skillet, scraping to loosen browned bits. Cook over high heat until reduced to about 2 tablespoons (30 ml). Add cream; cook until reduced by half. Add scallops and mustard; cook just until scallops are heated through. Add salt and pepper to taste.

PASTA PUTTANESCA

Serves 6
Preparation: 30 to 60 minutes

This traditional Italian dish is typically prepared with canned clams; fresh clams make an interesting and delicious variation. Parmesan cheese is not typically served with this dish.

1 onion, diced

1 red bell pepper, diced

1 green bell pepper, diced

1 small hot pepper, minced

Half of a head of garlic, peeled and minced

¼ cup (60 ml) olive oil

3 cups (540 g) diced tomatoes

1 cup (2.3 dl) dry white wine

½ cup (60 g) chopped kalamata olives

2 tablespoons (20 g) drained capers

3 pounds (1.36 kg) scrubbed clams

1 can (4 ounces/113 g) anchovies, drained and chopped

3 tablespoons (9 g) chopped fresh basil, or 1½ tablespoons (1.5 g) dried

3 tablespoons (7.5 g) fresh thyme, or 1½ tablespoons (5 g) dried

2 bay leaves

1 pound (454 g) packaged fettuccine

Salt and pepper

Begin heating large pot of salted water to boiling for cooking pasta. In large, heavy skillet that has a tight-fitting lid, sauté onion, red and green bell peppers, hot pepper and garlic in oil over medium-high heat until soft. Add tomatoes, wine, olives and capers and heat to boiling. Add clams. Cover tightly and steam just until clams open. Check your pan every couple of minutes and remove clams as they open, transferring to a dish and keeping warm. Discard any clams that haven't opened after about 5 minutes.

Add anchovies, basil, thyme and bay leaves to skillet. Cook over high heat until reduced by one-quarter. During this time, cook fettuccine according to package directions. While sauce and pasta are cooking, shuck clams if you would like; you may also leave them whole, in the shells. When sauce has reduced, return clams to skillet; add salt and pepper to taste. Toss sauce and clams with hot cooked fettuccine.

PAELLA

Serves 6 to 10
Preparation: Over 1 hour

Paella is one of the world's greatest peasant dishes. All manner of fish, shellfish and meats can be used. Don't be afraid to experiment using leftovers; they will only enhance your enjoyment of this dish.

1/2 pound (225 g) mushrooms, quartered

1 onion, diced

1 green bell pepper, diced

Half of a head of garlic, peeled and chopped

1/4 cup (60 ml) olive oil

2 cups (230 g) uncooked arborio or paella rice*

1 cup (180 g) diced tomatoes

2 cups (4.6 dl) hot chicken broth

2 cups (4.6 dl) hot fish stock (page 105)

2 bay leaves

2 teaspoons (.6 g) saffron threads

1 teaspoon (2 g) paprika

1 teaspoon (.9 g) chopped fresh basil

1/2 teaspoon (1 g) cayenne pepper

2 pounds (900 g) scrubbed clams

11/2 pounds (680 g) peeled and deveined raw shrimp

2 cups (180 g) cooked chicken and/or sausage, cut into 1-inch (2.5 cm) chunks (optional)

In Dutch oven or large flame-proof casserole, sauté mushrooms, onion, pepper and garlic in oil over medium heat for 3 to 4 minutes, until not quite soft. Add rice; sauté for an additional 3 minutes. Add tomatoes, chicken broth and fish stock; heat to boiling. As soon as mixture boils add bay leaves, saffron, paprika, basil and cayenne. Cover tightly, reduce heat to a simmer and cook, stirring occasionally, until rice is almost cooked through, 20 to 30 minutes. Place clams, shrimp and chicken on top of rice mixture; re-cover and cook for 5 to 6 minutes, until clams open up and shrimp is cooked through. Discard any clams that don't open.

*Arborio rice and paella rice are both short-grained, glutinous rice. Look for them at larger supermarkets, or at specialty Italian or Spanish stores.

PINEAPPLE SALSA

Sauces & Marinades

Sauces and marinades are the very soul of great seafood meals. At their best, they can bring out all the flavor or texture of your seafood. The key is to mate sauces or marinades to an appropriate fish. All too often a perfectly good sauce and a great piece of fish find themselves mismatched on a plate, with the result that we can't fully enjoy either fish or sauce. For example, I love the Chinese Black Bean Barbecue Sauce (page 92); however, the strong, spicy, sweet flavor needs seafood with a correspondingly assertive flavor to stand up to it.

Many professional chefs make the mistake of not tasting their sauce, however well constructed and tasty it may be, with the seafood they serve. The combination is often not nearly as good as it could or should be. So have fun, experiment and find sauce and seafood combinations that bring out the best in each other.

PINEAPPLE SALSA

About 4 cups (.95 l)
Preparation: Under 30 minutes

This great sauce is spectacular with almost any grilled fish; however, it may overpower very mild fish like halibut or cod.

1 pineapple, peeled, cored and cut into 1/2-inch-thick (1.25 cm) slices

1 tablespoon (15 ml) canola or other mild oil

1 red bell pepper, diced

1 green bell pepper, diced

1 red onion, diced

Leaves from half of a bunch of cilantro, minced

1 hot pepper, minced

Juice from 1 lemon

Juice from 1 lime

Brush pineapple on both sides with oil. Grill or sear in hot skillet until lightly brown on both sides. Dice finely and mix with all other ingredients in large bowl. You may serve this salsa right away, or refrigerate for up to a day.

REMOULADE SAUCE

Approximately 2³/₄ cups (6.3 dl)
Preparation: Under 15 minutes, plus 2 hours chilling

This great, easy sauce is perfect for any fried fish, and works equally well for a simple grilled fish like tuna or swordfish.

2 cups (510 g/4.6 dl) mayonnaise

1/4 cup (37 g) diced sweet bell peppers (any color)

1/4 cup (25 g) chopped green onions (white parts and half of the green parts)

Juice and zest from 2 lemons

2 tablespoons (30 g) coarse mustard

2 tablespoons (30 g) tomato paste

2 tablespoons (18 g) chopped dill pickle

2 tablespoons (5 g) chopped fresh basil

1 tablespoon (6 g) paprika

1 teaspoon (5 ml) Tabasco sauce

In mixing bowl, combine all ingredients. Cover and refrigerate for at least 2 hours, or overnight if possible.

GIN, GREEN PEPPERCORN AND CRANBERRY SAUCE

About 1 cup (2.3 dl)
Preparation: Under 30 minutes

This piquant version of a beurre blanc can be made 1 or 2 hours before serving; keep the sauce warm but not hot, or it may separate. Strong, assertively flavored grilled fish such as mackerel, bluefish or salmon are a good match for this sauce.

1/2 cup (1.2 dl) white wine

1/4 cup (60 ml) gin

1/4 cup (25 g) cooked cranberries

2 tablespoons (20 g) minced shallots

1 tablespoon (12 g) sugar

1 tablespoon (10 g) crushed green peppercorns

1/4 cup (55 g/half of a stick) unsalted butter, cut into 4 pieces

In medium saucepan, combine wine, gin, cranberries, shallots, sugar and green peppercorns; boil over medium-high heat until syrupy. Remove from heat; use wire whisk to beat in butter, a tablespoon at a time.

SPANISH ALMOND FENNEL SAUCE

About 1 1/2 cups (3.5 dl)
Preparation: Under 30 minutes

Serve this traditional Valencian sauce with relatively mild, flaky fish such as halibut, sole or haddock. It works well either on or underneath baked, broiled or sautéed fish.

1 cup (120 g) finely diced fennel

1 onion, julienned

6 cloves garlic, chopped

1/4 cup (60 ml) olive oil

1/4 cup plus 2 tablespoons (42 g) ground almonds

1 teaspoon (2 g) hot paprika

1 teaspoon (.3 g) dried oregano

1 teaspoon (.75 g) dried thyme

1 1/2 cups (3.5 dl) fish stock (page 105)

2 tablespoons (8 g) chopped flat-leaf (Italian) parsley

In large skillet, sauté fennel, onion and garlic in oil over low heat until soft but not browned. Add almonds, paprika, oregano and thyme; continue cooking until mixture is lightly browned. Add fish stock; increase heat to high and cook until reduced by two-thirds. Remove from heat; stir in parsley.

TERIYAKI SAUCE

About 1 1/2 cups (3.5 dl)
Preparation: Under 15 minutes, plus 1 hour steeping

Use as a marinade for any grilled or seared fish, or add near the end of cooking for any sautéed seafood such as shrimp or scallops.

3/4 cup (1.7 dl) orange juice

1/4 cup (60 ml) soy sauce

1/4 cup (60 ml) sherry

2 tablespoons (30 ml) rice vinegar

2 tablespoons (30 ml) honey or brown sugar

2 tablespoons (30 g) finely minced garlic

2 tablespoons (30 g) finely minced fresh gingerroot

In medium saucepan, combine all ingredients. Heat to boiling over medium heat, then remove from heat immediately. Set aside and allow to steep in pan for at least 1 hour.

CUCUMBER AND MUSTARD SAUCE

About 1 1/2 cups (3.5 dl)
Preparation: Under 15 minutes, plus 2 hours chilling

This mustard sauce is ideal for any smoked or pickled fish, and is superb with cured fish such as gravlax, herring or lox. It also makes a nice substitute cocktail sauce for shrimp.

Half of a cucumber, peeled, seeded and chopped

3 shallots, minced

Juice from 1 lemon

1/2 cup (128 g/1.2 dl) mayonnaise

1/2 cup (115 g/1.2 dl) sour cream

1/4 cup (13 g) snipped fresh dill weed

2 tablespoons (30 g) Dijon mustard

1/4 teaspoon (.5 g) white pepper

1/4 teaspoon (1.5 g) salt

In mixing bowl, combine all ingredients. Cover and refrigerate for at least 2 hours, or overnight if possible.

HARISSA

About 1 cup (2.3 dl)
Preparation: 30 to 60 minutes

This fiery condiment originated in Tunisia, where it is used to flavor stews. It makes an interesting accompaniment to grilled or broiled bluefish, swordfish, tuna or similar oily fish.

1 large onion, roughly chopped

1 head of garlic, cloves separated but not peeled

2 medium-sized hot peppers, such as jalapeño or serrano

1 carrot, peeled and roughly chopped

1 pound (454 g) roma tomatoes, roughly chopped

1/2 cup (1.2 dl) olive oil

1/2 teaspoon (1 g) caraway seed

1/2 teaspoon (1 g) ground cumin

1/2 teaspoon (3 g) salt

1/4 teaspoon (.5 g) pepper

Heat oven to 350°F (175°C). Combine all ingredients in medium roasting pan, stirring to combine. Roast until vegetables are very tender, 30 to 40 minutes, stirring several times. Allow to cool until just warm and run through food mill. Harissa will keep for at least 2 weeks refrigerated, and may be frozen for longer storage.

TAPENADE

TAPENADE

About 1 cup (2.3 dl)
Preparation: Under 15 minutes

This very strongly flavored Mediterranean sauce balances grilled fish perfectly. A little goes a long way, though; plan on about a tablespoon per serving.

1 cup (140 g) pitted kalamata olives

1 can (2 ounces/56.5 g) anchovy fillets

1 tablespoon (10 g) drained capers

Juice and zest from 1 lemon

3 cloves garlic, chopped

2 tablespoons (30 ml) olive oil

1 tablespoon (3 g) chopped fresh basil

1 tablespoon (4 g) chopped flat-leaf (Italian) parsley

¼ teaspoon (.5 g) pepper

Combine all ingredients in food processor fitted with metal blade. Pulse on-and-off until mixed together and roughly chopped.

TARTAR SAUCE

About 1½ cups (3.5 dl)
Preparation: Under 15 minutes

This classic tartar sauce fits perfectly with golden-brown fried fish. Every year when halibut season opens around the first of March, we fry a giant batch of cornmeal-breaded halibut and serve it to our employees with a big bowl of this tartar sauce.

1 cup (255 g/2.3 dl) mayonnaise

3 tablespoons (27 g) chopped dill pickles

2 tablespoons (25 g) finely diced onion

1 tablespoon (10 g) chopped drained capers

1 tablespoon (15 g) Dijon mustard

¼ teaspoon (.5 g) white pepper

¼ teaspoon (1.5 g) salt

Juice and zest from 1 lemon

Combine all ingredients in a medium bowl.

HAWAIIAN SESAME SEED SAUCE

CHINESE BLACK BEAN BARBECUE SAUCE

About 3 cups (6.9 dl)
Preparation: 30 to 60 minutes

Use this sauce as a marinade or stir-fry sauce. Check an Asian market for the fermented black beans.

¼ cup (60 g) minced fresh gingerroot

¼ cup (60 g) minced garlic

¼ cup (60 ml) dark sesame oil

1 package (8 ounces/225 g) Chinese fermented black beans, thoroughly rinsed

½ cup (1.2 dl) hoisin sauce

½ cup (1.2 dl) honey

¼ cup (60 ml) dry white wine

¼ cup (60 ml) dry sherry

¼ cup (60 ml) rice vinegar

2 tablespoons (30 ml) soy sauce

2 tablespoons (30 g) Asian chili-garlic paste

In large, heavy saucepan, sauté gingerroot and garlic in oil over medium heat until soft but not browned, 5 to 6 minutes. Add remaining ingredients; heat to boiling. Reduce heat so mixture simmers and cook for 30 minutes, stirring occasionally.

HAWAIIAN SESAME SEED SAUCE

About ¼ cup (60 ml)
Preparation: Under 15 minutes

This light, flavorful sauce can be served warm over cooked fish, or may be added to a hot pan with just-sautéed fish.

2 tablespoons (20 g) white sesame seed

¼ cup (60 ml) water

3 tablespoons (20 g) finely chopped green onions (white parts and half of the green parts)

2 tablespoons (30 ml) soy sauce

2 tablespoons (30 ml) dark sesame oil

1 tablespoon (15 g) finely minced fresh gingerroot

1 teaspoon (4 g) sugar

¼ teaspoon (.5 g) cayenne pepper

1 clove garlic, minced

In small, heavy skillet, toast sesame seeds over medium heat until light brown, being careful not to burn. Add all other ingredients and simmer over low heat until reduced by one-half.

BEURRE BLANC

About 2/3 cup (1.6 dl)
Preparation: Under 15 minutes

Beurre blanc (or white butter sauce) is the basis for many of the sauces served in white-tablecloth restaurants. For additional flavor, add chopped fresh herbs; for variety, substitute fruit juice for the wine. You may also choose to omit the cream although it does help stabilize the sauce. The sauce can be made 1 or 2 hours in advance; just keep it in a warm—but not hot—spot.

1/2 cup (1.2 dl) fish stock (page 105)

1/2 cup (1.2 dl) white wine

1 tablespoon (10 g) minced shallots

2 tablespoons (30 ml) cream

1/2 cup (110 g/1 stick) unsalted butter, cut into 8 pieces

In small saucepan, boil fish stock, wine and shallots over medium-high heat until reduced to 3 tablespoons (45 ml). Add cream and boil to reduce to 3 tablespoons once again. Remove from heat and whisk in butter, a piece at a time.

NOTE: IF THE SAUCE SHOULD SEPARATE BEFORE SERVING, MAKE ANOTHER REDUCTION OF WINE AND STOCK; WHEN THIS IS REDUCED TO 3 TABLESPOONS, REMOVE FROM HEAT AND CAREFULLY BEAT THE BROKEN SAUCE INTO THE NEW REDUCTION.

ROUILLE

About 2 cups (4.6 dl)
Preparation: Under 30 minutes

Rouille is traditionally used to top a crouton that will be placed on a serving of a fish soup such as Bouillabaisse (page 105). You may also use this purée to top grilled tuna or marlin steak.

1/2 cup (120 g) stale French bread cubes (crust removed before breaking or cutting into small chunks for measuring)

1 teaspoon (.3 g) saffron threads

Pinch of cayenne pepper

1/4 cup (60 ml) warm fish stock (page 105)

3 raw egg yolks (use yolks from commercially pasturized eggs for safety)

3 cloves garlic, minced

3/4 cup (1.8 dl) extra-virgin olive oil

1/4 cup (60 ml) canola oil

1 red bell pepper, roasted, peeled and seeded

1 tablespoon (15 g) tomato paste

1/2 teaspoon (3 g) salt

1/4 teaspoon (.5 g) black pepper

Place bread into bowl of food processor fitted with metal blade. Sprinkle with saffron and cayenne pepper; pour fish stock over bread and soak for a few minutes. Add egg yolks and garlic. Turn processor on, and, with motor running, add olive and canola oils in very thin stream through feed tube. When all oil has been incorporated, add red pepper, tomato paste, salt and pepper; process until well mixed.

TANDOORI-STYLE YOGURT MARINADE

About 1 1/4 cups (2.9 dl), enough for 2 to 3 pounds fish
Preparation: Under 15 minutes, plus 1 hour marinating

Cover your favorite fish or shellfish with this marinade and refrigerate for at least 1 hour. Brush off most of the marinade, oil the fish lightly and grill or bake. This marinade not only gives your fish a great, clean flavor, but also helps to keep it moist on the grill. Marlin, swordfish and shrimp all work beautifully prepared in this manner.

1 cup (2.3 dl) yogurt

2 tablespoons (30 g) roughly chopped fresh gingerroot

1 teaspoon (2 g) curry powder

1/2 teaspoon (1 g) ground cumin

1/4 teaspoon (.5 g) turmeric

1/4 teaspoon (.5 g) white pepper

1/4 teaspoon (1.5 g) salt

Leaves from 1 bunch of cilantro

4 cloves garlic, peeled

Juice and zest from 3 limes

Combine all ingredients in food processor fitted with metal blade. Pulse on-and-off until just mixed, 30 to 40 seconds.

PEACH, ONION AND PEPPER SALSA

About 1 1/2 cups (3.5 dl)
Preparation: 30 to 60 minutes

This spicy and flavorful salsa nicely complements oilier, firm-fleshed fish like salmon or swordfish.

2 large peaches, skinned and diced

Half of a red bell pepper, seeded and finely diced

Half of a jalapeño pepper, seeded and finely diced

1/4 cup (25 g) finely chopped green onions (white parts and half of the green parts)

2 tablespoons (30 ml) olive oil

2 tablespoons (5 g) chopped cilantro

1 tablespoon (15 ml) fresh lime juice

1 tablespoon (4 g) finely chopped flat-leaf (Italian) parsley

1/2 teaspoon (1 g) ground cumin

In mixing bowl, combine all ingredients. Cover and refrigerate for at least 30 minutes, to allow flavors to blend.

CHAPTER NINE

SALAD NIÇOISE

Side Dishes & Salads

I recently realized that even though I was a chef for ten years and have been a cooking instructor for twenty, I subsist mostly on fish and bread during the course of my working day. Like many colleagues in the business, I am content with a piece of seared fish and a chunk of bread. Of course, this isn't the way people eat in the real world (or, for that matter, the way I eat at home or at restaurants). In my cooking classes, people often ask the perfectly reasonable question, "What would you serve with...?"

Sides and salads should complement rather than overshadow your main course. A rich, intensely flavored seafood meal such as a fish curry begs for a simple steamed vegetable and rice. A light, simply sautéed halibut might allow for a more complex, heavier side dish such as a corn soufflé or wild rice pilaf. Following are some side dishes featuring seafood, and some all-time favorites to accompany the main event.

POKE

Serves 6 to 8
Preparation: Under 15 minutes, plus 1 hour marinating

Poke is a traditional salad served in Hawaii (it's also the name of a wild green that is popular in the South). The ingredients may vary but the salad is traditionally served on a bed of ogo, which is a very fine Hawaiian seaweed. Since ogo is hard to find outside Hawaii, you may serve this salad as is, or on a bed of shredded greens.

1 pound (454 g) frozen sashimi-grade tuna, thawed in refrigerator

1/2 cup (50 g) finely chopped green onions (white parts and half of the green parts)

2 tablespoons (30 ml) dark sesame oil

1 tablespoon (15 ml) soy sauce

1 teaspoon (5 g) finely minced fresh gingerroot

1/4 teaspoon (.5 g) cayenne pepper

2 cloves garlic, very finely minced

Cut tuna into 1/2-inch (1.25 cm) cubes and place in medium bowl. Add remaining ingredients and toss gently to mix. Cover and refrigerate for 1 to 2 hours.

SALAD NIÇOISE

Serves 4 to 6
Preparation: 30 to 60 minutes

This classic French salad makes a great lunch or light dinner. For a special presentation, compose each serving individually.

1/2 pound (225 g) skin-on new potatoes

1/2 pound (225 g) fresh green beans, rinsed, strings removed

1 head romaine lettuce, washed, dried and torn into 1- to 2-inch (2.5 to 5 cm) pieces

1 pound (454 g) cooked tuna,* broken into large chunks or flakes

1 can (8 ounces/225 g) artichoke hearts, drained and quartered

4 hard-boiled eggs, peeled and quartered

1/2 cup (90 g) quartered roma tomatoes

1/2 cup (70 g) pitted kalamata olives

1 small red onion, thinly sliced

VINAIGRETTE:

1/4 cup (60 ml) red wine vinegar

1 tablespoon (15 ml) lemon juice

1 teaspoon (4.5 g) coarse mustard

1/4 teaspoon (.5 g) pepper

3 cloves garlic, minced

1 cup (2.3 dl) olive oil

Heat large pot of water to boiling over high heat. Add potatoes; cook until just tender, 20 to 25 minutes. Meanwhile, heat a medium pot of water to boiling over high heat. Add green beans; cook for 3 minutes. Drain beans and refresh briefly under cold, running water; set aside. When potatoes are tender, drain and refresh under cold, running water; cut into quarters.

Spread torn romaine leaves out on large platter. Decoratively arrange potatoes, green beans, tuna, artichoke hearts, eggs, tomatoes, olives and onion on top of lettuce. For vinaigrette, combine vinegar, lemon juice, mustard, pepper and garlic in small bowl; whisk to blend. While whisking steadily, slowly add oil, whisking until dressing has emulsified. Just before serving, drizzle dressing over salad; serve immediately.

*THE TUNA CAN BE GRILLED, BAKED OR BROILED SPECIALLY FOR THIS DISH, OR CAN BE PREPARED DURING THE COURSE OF ANOTHER MEAL AND RESERVED.

COLD OCTOPUS SALAD

Serves 6 to 8
Preparation: Over 1 hour

This salad will actually improve if allowed to marinate overnight, tossing occasionally.

1 gallon (3.8 l) water

1 cleaned octopus (2 to 3 pounds/900 g to 1.36 kg)

1 red onion, julienned

1 green bell pepper, julienned

1 red bell pepper, julienned

1/2 cup (1.2 dl) olive oil

3 tablespoons (45 ml) lemon juice

1 tablespoon (15 ml) balsamic vinegar

3 cloves garlic, minced

3 tablespoons (8 g) chopped fresh cilantro or flat-leaf (Italian) parsley

1/2 teaspoon (3 g) salt

1/4 teaspoon (.5 g) pepper

In stockpot or large saucepan, heat water to boiling over high heat. Add octopus and return to boiling. As soon as water boils, reduce to a simmer and poach for 1 to 1 1/4 hours. Drain octopus; refrigerate until cool, at least 30 minutes.

Slice octopus thinly (approximately 1/4 inch/.6 cm thick) and combine in large bowl with all other ingredients. Toss to mix well, return to refrigerator and allow to marinate for at least 2 hours before serving.

ROAST ASPARAGUS

Serves 4
Preparation: Under 15 minutes

1 pound (454 g) thin asparagus

1/2 cup (1.2 dl) water

3 tablespoons (45 ml) olive oil

2 tablespoons (30 ml) balsamic vinegar

1 teaspoon (6 g) salt

1/2 teaspoon (.5 g) pepper

Heat oven to 450°F (230°C). Trim and discard the bottom 1 1/2 inches (3.75 cm) from each asparagus spear. Lay asparagus on baking sheet, spreading out evenly. Combine water, oil, vinegar, salt and pepper in small bowl, whisking to blend. Pour dressing over asparagus. Roast for 8 to 12 minutes, until just tender.

SOUTHERN GARLIC GREENS

Serves 4 to 8
Preparation: 30 to 60 minutes

1/4 pound (113 g) sliced bacon, cut into 1/4-inch (.6 cm) pieces

2 pounds (900 g) greens (mustard, kale, turnip or others), stems removed, well washed

1 onion, diced

4 cloves garlic, chopped

1/4 cup (60 ml) water

2 tablespoons (30 ml) lemon juice

1/4 teaspoon (.5 g) cayenne pepper

1/4 teaspoon (.5 g) black pepper

1/4 teaspoon (1.5 g) salt

In large, heavy skillet, sauté bacon over medium heat until not quite crisp; meanwhile, cut greens into 1- to 2-inch (2.5 to 5 cm) pieces and set aside. When bacon is beginning to crisp, add onion and sauté until soft, about 3 minutes. Add garlic; sauté for 1 minute longer. Add greens, water, lemon juice, cayenne, black pepper and salt. Cook for 10 to 15 minutes, or until greens are tender; add a little more water if greens become too dry during cooking.

HUSH PUPPIES

Serves 4 to 6
Preparation: Under 30 minutes

These delicious southern-fried biscuits are a perfect accompaniment to any fried fish or perhaps a seafood gumbo.

3 cups (6.9 dl) canola or other mild oil

1 cup (160 g) cornmeal

1/4 cup (35 g) all-purpose flour

2 teaspoons (8 g) sugar

1 teaspoon (3.7 g) baking powder

1 teaspoon (4.3 g) baking soda

1/2 teaspoon (3 g) salt

1/4 teaspoon (.5 g) pepper

1 egg

1/2 cup (1.2 dl) milk

2 tablespoons (30 ml) buttermilk

2 tablespoons (20 g) finely minced shallots

In large pot or deep-fryer, begin heating oil over medium-high heat. Meanwhile, in large bowl, stir together cornmeal, flour, sugar, baking powder, baking soda, salt and pepper. Sift cornmeal mixture into another large bowl. In medium bowl, whisk together egg, milk, buttermilk and shallots. Quickly but gently whisk liquids into dry ingredients until barely mixed (it is better to slightly under-mix than risk over-mixing). When oil has heated to 375°F (190°C), use spoon to carefully drop batter in 1-inch-wide (2.5 cm) balls into hot oil; fry until golden brown. Drain on paper towels; serve immediately.

SEARED YELLOWTAIL AND SPRING GREENS SALAD

Serves 4 to 6
Preparation: Under 30 minutes

Yellowtail, which is often called hamachi, is a member of the jack family and one of the world's most treasured fish. Prized by sport anglers, yellowtail is also a major commercial species that is sold all over the world as one of the most popular species for sushi. The rich, oily and yet delicate meat lends itself to a host of different cooking methods.

1/2 teaspoon (3 g) salt

1/4 teaspoon (.5 g) pepper

1/4 teaspoon (.5 g) ground cumin

1 pound (454 g) boneless, skinless yellowtail, cut into 1/2-inch (1.25 cm) cubes

1/4 cup plus 2 tablespoons (90 ml) olive oil, divided

2 tablespoons (30 ml) balsamic vinegar

1 tablespoon (15 ml) lemon juice

1 teaspoon (4.5 g) Dijon mustard

2 tablespoons (5 g) minced fresh basil or tarragon

8 cups (440 g) spring mix salad greens

In mixing bowl, stir together salt, pepper and cumin. Toss yellowtail cubes with this seasoning until evenly coated. In large, heavy skillet, heat 2 tablespoons (30 ml) of the oil over medium-high heat until shimmering. Add seasoned fish; sauté for 3 to 4 minutes, until barely cooked through. Lift out fish and transfer to small bowl; set aside to cool to warm room temperature.

In large salad bowl, whisk together vinegar, lemon juice, mustard, basil and remaining 1/4 cup (60 ml) oil. Add greens; toss gently. Arrange warm yellowtail over greens; serve immediately.

APPLE, BLUE CHEESE AND PECAN SALAD

Serves 4
Preparation: Under 30 minutes

4 cups (220 g) mixed salad greens

2 firm, tart apples,* peeled, cored and diced

1/2 cup (53 g) coarsely chopped pecans

8 ounces (225 g) good-quality blue cheese, crumbled

FRUIT VINAIGRETTE:

2 tablespoons (30 ml) orange juice

1 tablespoon (15 ml) balsamic vinegar

1 tablespoon (15 ml) lemon juice

1 teaspoon (4.5 g) Dijon mustard

1/4 teaspoon (.5 g) pepper

1 shallot, minced

3 tablespoons (45 ml) canola or other mild oil

3 tablespoons (45 g) olive oil

In medium salad bowl, combine greens, apples, pecans and blue cheese; toss gently. For fruit vinaigrette, combine orange juice, vinegar, lemon juice, mustard, pepper and shallot in small bowl; whisk to blend. While whisking steadily, slowly add canola and olive oils, whisking until dressing has emulsified. Just before serving, pour dressing over salad; toss gently and serve immediately.

*IF YOU ARE GOING TO WAIT A WHILE BEFORE DRESSING AND SERVING THE SALAD, SPRINKLE THE APPLES WITH A LITTLE LEMON JUICE SO THEY DON'T TURN BROWN.

ROASTED NEW POTATOES

Serves 4 to 6
Preparation: 30 to 60 minutes

2 pounds (900 g) new potatoes, rinsed, dried and cut into 1/2-inch (1.25 cm) chunks

1 head of garlic, cloves separated but not peeled

1/4 cup (60 ml) olive oil

1 tablespoon (2 g) fresh whole rosemary leaves

1 teaspoon (6 g) salt

1/4 teaspoon (.5 g) pepper

Heat oven to 475°F (245°C). Combine all ingredients in large cast-iron pan or on baking sheet, stirring to coat potatoes with oil. Bake for 20 to 30 minutes, or until crisp, brown and cooked through.

GARLIC MASHED POTATOES

Serves 6 to 8
Preparation: 30 to 60 minutes

3 pounds (1.36 kg) Yukon gold potatoes, peeled and cut in half

1/2 cup (1.2 dl) cream

1/4 cup (55 g/half of a stick) butter

Half of a head of garlic, peeled and roughly chopped

1/4 cup (60 ml) warm milk

1 teaspoon (6 g) salt

1/2 teaspoon (1 g) white pepper

Place potatoes in large pot; cover generously with water. Heat to boiling over high heat. Cook until tender, 25 to 30 minutes. Meanwhile, combine cream, butter and garlic in small, heavy saucepan. Simmer over low heat for 20 minutes, or until garlic is soft. When potatoes are tender, drain well; return to dry pot and allow steam to escape for a couple of minutes. Add cream mixture, milk, salt and pepper and mash with potato masher; alternately, you may rice in potato ricer, or mash in electric stand mixer.

WARM GREEN BEAN AND HAZELNUT SALAD

Serves 4 to 6
Preparation: 30 to 60 minutes

1 pound (454 g) fresh green beans, rinsed, strings removed

2 hard-boiled eggs, peeled and roughly chopped

1/2 cup (68 g) whole hazelnuts, toasted, peeled and chopped (see page 58)

2 roma tomatoes, finely diced

1/4 cup plus 1 tablespoon (75 ml) olive oil

2 tablespoons (30 ml) lemon juice

1 teaspoon (4.5 g) Dijon mustard

1/2 teaspoon (1 g) pepper

1 clove garlic, minced

Heat large pot of water to boiling over high heat. Add green beans; cook for 3 minutes. Drain beans and refresh briefly under cold, running water; beans should still be warm. Place drained beans in large, shallow bowl. Garnish with chopped egg, hazelnuts and tomatoes. In medium bowl, whisk together oil, lemon juice, mustard, pepper and garlic; drizzle over beans.

SAFFRON RICE

Serves 4 to 6
Preparation: Under 30 minutes

This is an easy and delicious side dish for any meal. I probably make saffron rice once every two to three weeks.

1 small onion, finely diced

2 tablespoons (30 ml) olive oil

1 1/2 cups (235 g) uncooked basmati rice

2 1/4 cups (5.2 dl) water

1 teaspoon (.3 g) saffron threads

1 teaspoon (6 g) salt

In medium saucepan that has a tight-fitting lid, sauté onion in oil over medium-low heat until soft and translucent. Add rice and sauté for 2 to 3 minutes longer. Add water, saffron and salt. Increase heat to high; cover and heat to boiling. Immediately reduce heat so liquid is simmering; cook for 12 to 15 minutes. Fluff rice and serve.

POLENTA

Serves 6 to 8
Preparation: Over 1 hour

The polenta may be cooked and refrigerated a day or two in advance, and simply reheated before serving.

5 cups (1.2 l) water

2 tablespoons (30 ml) olive oil

1 teaspoon (.3 g) saffron threads

1 teaspoon (6 g) salt

1½ cups (270 g) polenta

¼ cup (30 g) grated Parmesan cheese

In large saucepan, heat water, oil, saffron and salt to boiling over medium-high heat; meanwhile, lightly oil baking dish or baking sheet and set aside. Gradually whisk polenta into boiling water; reduce heat to simmer and cook for 20 minutes, stirring constantly. Remove from heat; add Parmesan cheese and stir just until mixed. Pour polenta into prepared dish. Refrigerate for at least 30 minutes, or as long as a day (cover dish with plastic wrap after polenta is cool if refrigerating longer than 30 minutes). You may then cut polenta into any size pieces you wish and grill, fry or bake until heated through.

FRIED PLANTAINS

Serves 4 to 6
Preparation: Under 15 minutes

Plantains are a starchy relative of the banana; unlike bananas, they require cooking, and are usually fried or boiled. Plantains are a staple starch in many Caribbean countries, and are a perfect side dish to a simple grilled fish with a salsa or fruit salsa.

¼ cup plus 2 tablespoons (90 ml) canola or other mild oil

3 ripe plantains, peeled and diagonally sliced ¼ inch (.6 cm) thick

2 tablespoons (27 g) brown sugar

1 tablespoon (15 ml) lime juice

½ teaspoon (3 g) salt

¼ teaspoon (.5 g) pepper

In large, heavy skillet, heat oil over medium heat. When oil is hot but not smoking, add plantains and fry for 3 to 4 minutes per side, until tender and browned. Add brown sugar, lime juice, salt and pepper to skillet; toss gently to combine.

WILD RICE PILAF

Serves 4 to 6
Preparation: Over 1 hour

1 small onion, diced

½ pound (225 g) mushrooms, quartered

¼ cup (34 g) whole hazelnuts, toasted, peeled and chopped (see page 58)

2 tablespoons (30 ml) olive oil

1 tablespoon (15 g) butter

1 cup (180 g) uncooked wild rice

1 quart (.95 l) water or chicken broth

1 teaspoon (6 g) salt

¼ teaspoon (.5 g) pepper

In medium saucepan, sauté onion, mushrooms and hazelnuts in oil and butter over medium heat for 3 to 4 minutes. Add wild rice; sauté for 1 minute longer. Add water, salt and pepper and cover tightly. As soon as it comes to a boil, reduce heat to simmer and cook for 40 to 45 minutes.

BALSAMIC CAESAR SALAD

Serves 6 to 8
Preparation: Under 30 minutes

1 head romaine lettuce, washed, dried and torn into 1- to 2-inch (2.5 to 5 cm) pieces

1 cup (40 g) croutons

1 egg (use yolks from commercially pasteurized eggs for safety)

3 cloves garlic

½ cup (63 g) grated Parmesan cheese

2 tablespoons (30 ml) lemon juice

2 tablespoons (30 ml) balsamic vinegar

2 teaspoons (18 g) coarse mustard

¼ teaspoon (.5 g) pepper

¼ cup (60 ml) olive oil

¼ cup (60 ml) canola oil

In large salad bowl, toss together lettuce and croutons. In food processor fitted with metal blade, combine egg, garlic, Parmesan cheese, lemon juice, vinegar, mustard and pepper. Turn processor on, and, with motor running, add olive and canola oils in very thin stream through feed tube until all oil has been incorporated and dressing has emulsified. Pour dressing over lettuce; toss and serve immediately.

CHAPTER TEN

THAI SHRIMP SOUP

Soups & Chowders

As I am writing this at my home in Minneapolis, it is -10°F (-23°C) outside today, and I can think of nothing more soothing than sitting down to a big bowl of rich Bouillabaisse (page 105). Soups make a great first course, lunch or light dinner. The soups in this chapter run the gamut from rich, creamy main courses like Scallop and Corn Chowder (page 101) to light, bright, spicy Thai Shrimp Soup (page 101). Most can successfully be made ahead of time; prepare the base, without the seafood, and refrigerate until close to serving time. When you're almost ready to serve, reheat the base, add the seafood, and finish cooking as directed.

SCALLOP AND CORN CHOWDER

Serves 4 to 6
Preparation: 30 to 60 minutes

1/4 pound (113 g) sliced bacon, cut into 1/4-inch (.6 cm) pieces	1 bay leaf
1 large onion, diced	2 cups (330 g) corn kernels (from about 8 ears fresh corn)
1 rib celery, diced	1 cup (2.3 dl) cream
2 shallots, minced	1 pound (454 g) bay scallops
1 clove garlic, chopped	1 teaspoon (6 g) salt
1 cup (155 g) diced, skin-on potatoes (1/4-inch/.6 cm dice)	1 teaspoon (2 g) white pepper
3 cups (6.9 dl) fish stock (page 105)	1/4 teaspoon (.5 g) cayenne pepper
1 cup (2.3 dl) dry white wine	

In large, heavy saucepan, sauté bacon over medium heat until almost crisp. Add onion, celery, shallots and garlic; sauté for 3 to 4 minutes longer. Add potatoes, fish stock, wine and bay leaf. Heat to boiling; adjust heat so mixture boils gently and cook until potatoes are almost tender, about 15 minutes. Reduce heat to low; add corn, cream, scallops, salt, and white and cayenne peppers. Simmer until scallops are just cooked through, 4 to 5 minutes.

THAI SHRIMP SOUP

Serves 4 to 6
Preparation: 30 to 60 minutes

The lemongrass adds a wonderful flavor to this soup. Alert your guests that the lemongrass is too tough to chew, however; it is usually sucked on briefly, then discreetly discarded onto the side of the soup plate.

2 quarts (1.9 l) shrimp, lobster or fish stock (page 105), or chicken broth

3 stalks fresh lemongrass, split and diagonally cut into 1-inch (2.5 cm) pieces*

4 Kaffir lime leaves**, optional

Juice and zest from 2 limes

1 hot pepper, minced

1 tablespoon (14 g) tamarind paste**

1 tablespoon (15 ml) Thai fish sauce (nam pla)**

Leaves from 1 bunch of cilantro, chopped

1 bunch of green onions, minced (white and green parts)

1 1/4 pounds (570 g) peeled and deveined raw shrimp

1/2 cup (1.2 dl) coconut milk

In small stockpot or large saucepan, heat stock to boiling over high heat. Add lemongrass, lime leaves, lime juice and zest, hot pepper, tamarind paste and fish sauce. Heat to boiling; cook until reduced by half, 15 to 20 minutes. Add cilantro, green onions and shrimp; reduce heat and simmer until shrimp are cooked through, 3 to 4 minutes. Stir in coconut milk and serve immediately.

*YOU MAY SUBSTITUTE 1 TEASPOON (2 G) GRATED LEMON RIND FOR THE LEMONGRASS.

**LOOK FOR THESE THAI STAPLES AT AN ASIAN SPECIALTY STORE; FISH SAUCE CAN ALSO BE FOUND AT MANY LARGE SUPERMARKETS. IF THE TAMARIND PASTE LOOKS STRINGY AND HAS SEEDS, BLEND WITH A SMALL AMOUNT OF WATER, THEN STRAIN OUT SEEDS AND COARSE MATERIAL BEFORE USING.

NEW ENGLAND CLAM CHOWDER

Serves 6 to 8
Preparation: 30 to 60 minutes

1/4 pound (113 g) sliced bacon, cut into 1/4-inch (.6 cm) pieces

1 large onion, diced

1 carrot, diced

1 rib celery, diced

2 tablespoons (30 g) butter

2 tablespoons (15 g) all-purpose flour

1 quart (.95 l) fish stock (page 105)

2 cups (310 g) diced skin-on potatoes (1/4-inch/.6 cm dice)

1 teaspoon (.75 g) dried thyme

1 teaspoon (.5 g) dried tarragon

1/2 teaspoon (.4 g) dried marjoram

1/2 teaspoon (1 g) white pepper

2 bay leaves

1 cup (2.3 dl) white wine

3 pounds (1.36 kg) scrubbed clams

1 cup (2.3 dl) cream

In large saucepan, sauté bacon over medium heat until almost browned. Pour off as much bacon grease as possible, then add onion, carrot, celery and butter to pan. Sauté vegetables for 5 minutes. Sprinkle flour into pan, stirring constantly; cook for 3 minutes longer. Add stock, potatoes, thyme, tarragon, marjoram, pepper and bay leaves. Cook until potatoes are just tender, 15 to 20 minutes.

Meanwhile, in separate saucepan that has a tight-fitting lid, heat wine to boiling over medium-high heat. Add clams; cover tightly and steam just until clams open. Check your pan every couple of minutes and remove clams as they open, transferring to a dish and keeping warm. Discard any clams that don't open after 6 to 8 minutes. Carefully pour clam cooking liquid into soup, withholding any settled sand. Shuck clams, discarding shells; chop clam meat if you like, or leave clams whole. When potatoes are tender, stir in cream and clam meats.

BILLI-BI (FRENCH MUSSEL STEW)

Serves 4
Preparation: Under 30 minutes

According to one popular account, this classic French soup was named after William B. (Billy) Leeds, a tin tycoon who frequently requested the dish at the famous Maxim's restaurant in Paris.

2 cloves garlic, minced

1/4 cup (55 g/half of a stick) butter

1 cup (2.3 dl) white wine

2 pounds (900 g) fresh, live mussels, scrubbed, beards removed (page 28)

1 1/2 cups (3.5 dl) cream

1/2 teaspoon (.15 g) saffron threads

2 tablespoons (30 ml) dry sherry

1/2 teaspoon (3 g) salt

1/4 teaspoon (.5 g) white pepper

In large saucepan that has a tight-fitting lid, sauté garlic in butter over low heat until soft but not brown. Add wine and mussels; increase heat to high and cover pan tightly. Steam just until mussels open. Check your pan every couple of minutes and remove mussels as they open, transferring to a dish and keeping warm. Discard any mussels that don't open after about 5 minutes.

Continue cooking wine mixture until reduced by one-half; meanwhile, shuck cooked mussels, discarding shells. When wine mixture has reduced, add cream and saffron; reduce heat to medium and cook for 3 to 4 minutes. Stir in sherry, salt, pepper and reserved mussel meats; serve immediately.

SIMPLE BONITO OR TUNA CHOWDER

Serves 4
Preparation: 30 to 60 minutes

1 pound (454 g) bonito or tuna steaks

1/2 cup (1.2 dl) olive oil

1 large onion, diced

3 cloves garlic, roughly chopped

1 quart (.95 l) fish stock (page 105)

1 cup (2.3 dl) white wine

1 cup (180 g) diced tomatoes

4 new potatoes, quartered

1 bay leaf

1 teaspoon (.3 g) dried basil

1 teaspoon (6 g) salt

1/2 teaspoon (.4 g) dried marjoram

1/2 teaspoon (.4 g) dried thyme

1/2 teaspoon (1 g) pepper

3 tablespoons (12 g) chopped fresh flat-leaf (Italian) parsley

Remove and discard skin, bones, and any bloodline from fish steaks; cut fish into 3/4-inch (1.9 cm) cubes. Heat oil in large, heavy saucepan over medium-high heat until shimmering. Add fish cubes; sauté for 3 to 4 minutes. Use slotted spoon to transfer fish to bowl; set aside and keep warm.

Add onion to pan; sauté for 3 to 4 minutes, or until soft. Add garlic; sauté for an additional minute. Add stock, wine, tomatoes, potatoes, bay leaf, basil, salt, marjoram, thyme and pepper. Reduce heat to low and simmer until potatoes are cooked through, approximately 15 minutes. Stir in bonito chunks and parsley; serve immediately.

SEAFOOD GUMBO

Serves 8 to 10
Preparation: Over 1 hour

If you would like to make this gumbo in advance, prepare it up to the point of adding the seafood, then cool and refrigerate for up to 2 days. The flavor of the gumbo actually improves as it sits. You may also choose to add spicy sausage such as andouille to the gumbo; some people add cooked chicken or diced fish also.

½ cup (1.2 dl) canola or other mild oil, divided

¼ cup (35 g) all-purpose flour

1 large onion, diced

2 ribs celery, diced

½ cup (75 g) diced green bell pepper

½ cup (75 g) diced red bell pepper

6 cloves garlic, chopped

1½ quarts (1.4 l) fish stock (page 105)

1 cup (2.3 dl) white wine

1 cup (100 g) sliced okra

1 cup (180 g) diced tomatoes

3 bay leaves

1 teaspoon (.75 g) dried thyme

1 teaspoon (.3 g) dried oregano

1 teaspoon (6 g) salt

½ teaspoon (1 g) black pepper

¼ teaspoon (.5 g) cayenne pepper

1 pint (575 g) shucked oysters, with their liquor

1 pound (454 g) claw crabmeat

1 pound (454 g) peeled and deveined raw shrimp

Hot cooked rice

In small, heavy sauté pan, whisk ¼ cup (60 ml) of the oil with the flour until smooth. Cook this roux over medium heat, stirring constantly, until roux is shiny and dark brown.* Be careful not to let it burn or turn black. Remove browned roux from heat; set aside.

In small stockpot or large saucepan, sauté onion, celery, green and red peppers and garlic in remaining ¼ cup (60 ml) oil over medium heat until vegetables begin to soften. Add stock, wine, okra, tomatoes, bay leaves, thyme, oregano, salt, and black and cayenne peppers; heat to boiling. Boil for 10 to 15 minutes, then slowly whisk in browned roux. Reduce heat so mixture simmers and cook for 5 minutes longer. Add oysters with their liquor, crabmeat and shrimp; simmer until seafood is cooked through, about 5 minutes. Serve immediately over rice.

*IF YOU PREFER, PLACE WHISKED ROUX MIXTURE IN SMALL DISH AND BROWN IN A 350°F (175°C) OVEN, STIRRING OCCASIONALLY.

MANHATTAN-STYLE CLAM CHOWDER

OYSTER STEW

Serves 4
Preparation: Under 15 minutes

1/4 cup (55 g/half of a stick) butter

1 pint (575 g) shucked oysters, with their liquor

2 cups (4.6 dl) cream

1 cup (2.3 dl) milk

1/2 teaspoon (3 g) salt

1/4 teaspoon (.5 g) white pepper

1/4 teaspoon (1.2 ml) Tabasco sauce

In medium saucepan, melt butter over high heat. When butter is foaming, add oysters with their liquor; sauté for 3 to 4 minutes, until edges of oysters begin to curl. Add cream, milk, salt, pepper and Tabasco; reduce heat and simmer until hot.

MANHATTAN-STYLE CLAM CHOWDER

Serves 4 to 6
Preparation: 30 to 60 minutes

2 large onions, diced

1 cup (150 g) diced green bell pepper

1 cup (150 g) diced red bell pepper

4 cloves garlic, chopped

1/4 cup (60 ml) olive oil

1 cup (2.3 dl) white wine

1 teaspoon (.3 g) dried basil

1 teaspoon (.75 g) dried marjoram

1 teaspoon (.3 g) dried oregano

2 bay leaves

3 pounds (1.36 kg) scrubbed clams

1 quart (.95 l) fish stock (page 105)

1 cup (180 g) diced tomatoes

1 cup (155 g) diced, skin-on potatoes (1/4-inch/.6 cm dice)

In large saucepan that has a tight-fitting lid, sauté onions, red and green peppers, and garlic in oil over medium heat for 4 to 5 minutes. Add wine, basil, marjoram, oregano and bay leaves; heat to boiling. Add clams. Cover tightly and steam just until clams open. Check your pan every couple of minutes and remove clams as they open, transferring to a dish and keeping warm. Discard any clams that don't open after 6 to 8 minutes.

Add fish stock, tomatoes and potatoes to pan. Reduce heat to low and simmer for 15 to 20 minutes, or until potatoes are just tender. Meanwhile, shuck cooked clams and chop clam meats roughly; discard shells. Just before serving, stir clam meats into chowder.

BOUILLABAISSE

Serves 6 to 8
Preparation: Over 1 hour

Although bouillabaisse has a reputation for being too difficult—or too elegant—for the home cook, it originated as a peasant seafood stew. I like to make the base for the bouillabaisse ahead of time—in fact, even a couple of days ahead is fine. Just buy fresh fish the day you are going to finish it. You may use virtually any combination of fish and shellfish in the bouillabaisse—scallops, shrimp and a variety of fish work great. Bouillabaisse is traditionally served with Rouille (page 93).

BASE:

1 large onion, diced

Half of a head of fennel, diced (or 3 ribs celery, diced)

3 leeks, cleaned and sliced (white parts only)

8 cloves garlic, chopped

1/2 cup (75 g) diced red bell pepper

1/2 cup (75 g) diced green bell pepper

1 cup (2.3 dl) olive oil

2 quarts (1.9 l) fish stock (page 105)

1 cup (2.3 dl) white wine

2 cups (360 g) diced tomatoes

1 teaspoon (.3 g) saffron threads

1 teaspoon (.3 g) dried basil

1 teaspoon (.75 g) dried thyme

1 teaspoon (.75 g) dried marjoram

2 bay leaves

Juice and zest from 1 orange

2 pounds (900 g) scrubbed clams

2 pounds (900 g) fresh, live mussels, scrubbed, beards removed (page 28)

2 pounds (900 g) boneless, skinless grouper, monkfish or other firm white fish, cut into 1-inch (2.5 cm) cubes

In small stockpot or large saucepan that has a tight-fitting lid, sauté onion, fennel, leeks, garlic, and red and green peppers in oil over medium heat until soft, 4 to 5 minutes. Add remaining base ingredients; increase heat to high and boil until reduced by one-third, approximately 15 minutes. Bouillabaisse may be prepared to this point a day or two before serving; cool and refrigerate for storage, or proceed immediately with final cooking.

For final cooking, reheat base if necessary. Add clams and mussels; cover tightly. Cook until clams and mussels open, 5 to 8 minutes; discard any clams or mussels that have not opened. Add fish and continue to cook, covered, until fish is cooked through, approximately 8 minutes longer.

FISH STOCK

About 6 cups
Preparation: 30 to 60 minutes

Any part of the fish except the gills and the viscera may be used to make a fish stock, or fumet. Crab and shrimp shells add flavor, as do shrimp heads. Fish stocks do not need to cook nearly as long as meat stocks because the bones render their flavor quickly. I like to keep stock in my freezer at all times; it's ideal for steaming fish or shellfish, and is frequently used as the basis for a soup or stew. I pour the warm fish stock into ice-cube trays, cool a bit, and then freeze. Once frozen, the cubes can be put in a plastic bag until needed.

2 to 3 pounds (900 g to 1.36 kg) fish frames and trimmings

1 1/2 quarts (1.4 l) cold water

1 cup (2.3 dl) white wine

2 ribs celery, chopped

1 large onion, chopped

1 carrot, chopped

2 bay leaves

1 teaspoon (.75 g) dried thyme

1 teaspoon (.75 g) dried marjoram

10 whole peppercorns (black, white or mixed-color)

Rinse fish parts well and place all ingredients in a stockpot or large saucepan. Heat to boiling over high heat. As soon as stock boils, reduce heat and simmer, uncovered, for 30 minutes. While stock is simmering, carefully skim and discard the foam from the top every 5 minutes or so (this will yield a nice, clean stock). Strain and cool before refrigerating or freezing.*

*FOR MORE INTENSE FLAVOR, THE STRAINED STOCK MAY BE REDUCED FURTHER IF DESIRED.

Variation: Shellfish Stock

Substitute 2 to 3 pounds (900 g to 1.36 kg) shrimp shells and heads, lobster shells, crab shells, or any combination, for the fish frames and trimmings. Proceed as directed.

CHAPTER ELEVEN

Preserving & Cooking with Preserved Seafood

Most cooking methods have come about not with long hours experimenting in fancy restaurants but rather as responses to conditions or challenges. Many Asian foods, for instance, use dried preserved foods because their cuisines developed without the benefit of refrigeration or artificial preservatives.

In the past, if you wanted to enjoy seafood in landlocked areas far from the ocean you simply had no choice other than preserved seafood. Smoking, pickling, salting, canning and drying were developed by necessity (which really is the mother of invention). These techniques have given us a rich culinary legacy, including dishes such as Ceviche (page 111), Gravlax (page 111) and Brandade (page 114).

Following are basic instructions for the three types of preserving that are most commonly done by the home cook: smoking, pickling and salting. Some of the recipes that follow illustrate the various techniques, while others use preserved seafood such as smoked fish or commercially dried cod—a common staple in Mediterranean cooking.

Smoking

Probably the most common home-preservation technique is smoking. There are two basic types of smoking: cold smoking and hot smoking. Both of these methods preserve fish and can add great flavor as well. Cold smoking is done at a low temperature, between 80°F and 90°F (20°C to 32°C), for a relatively long period of time—anywhere from 12 to 48 hours. Hot smoking (also called smoke-cooking) is done at a much higher temperature, usually from 160°F to 300°F (70°C to 150°C), for a much shorter period of time, generally from 1 to 4 hours.

Both cold and hot smoking start with brining, a salting process that removes moisture from the fish,

allowing the smoke to more easily penetrate into the flesh. Brining also helps kill potentially harmful parasites, and keeps bacteria in check.

Cold smoking is actually a curing process. It can be quite tricky, and is usually reserved for commercial applications. Time, temperature, humidity and the salinity of the brine all must be tightly controlled to ensure quality and safety. A good example of cold-smoked fish is lox (sometimes called nova lox), a lightly salted and lightly smoked salmon with a delicate, buttery texture and a mild smoky flavor.

Hot smoking is much easier for the amateur, and is a delicious way to cook fish. Oily fish such as salmon, mackerel and tuna tend to work best for hot smoking; their flesh and flavor can hold up to the strong flavor of smoking, and their oiliness helps keep the final product moist. Many experienced cooks prefer to smoke fish that has been previously frozen. It seems to accept smoke more readily than fresh fish, but either may be used.

There are many different varieties of smokers, ranging from thermostatically controlled electric smokers, to charcoal kettle grills, to homemade smokers constructed from garbage cans, old refrigerators or clean oil drums. All have their advantages. If you do a fair amount of smoking it may be worth the modest investment for an electric smoker. They offer precise temperature control and are relatively airtight, which allows for the easy manipulation of the smoke concentration.

On the other hand if you, like me, smoke fish only occasionally, a covered kettle grill and some wood chips work just fine. For the most flavor, use a small amount of charcoal rather than the amount you'd use for normal grilling; this cooler heat level allows you to smoke the fish for a longer time. Arrange a small handful of briquettes on each side of the grill, leaving the center area open. Place a pan of water between the coals; this helps keep the fish moist. After brining the fish, place it on the grate over the pan of water; toss a few soaked chunks of wood onto the coals, cover the grill, and smoke until the fish is cooked. Hot-smoked fish should be cooked to an internal temperature of at least 160°F (70°C). Properly smoked fish will keep at least a week under refrigeration; and since hot smoking fully cooks the fish, you don't need to worry about potentially harmful parasites that may have been in the fish.

Apple, alder, hickory, maple and mesquite are the most popular woods used for smoking, although even common material such as corn cobs, pecan shells and grape vines work well. Try experimenting with various woods for different flavor combinations.

You may also add spices such as dill, thyme or cinnamon to the brine to help influence the flavor of the smoked fish. You can use the basic recipe for hot-smoked salmon (page 109) as a starting point for your own smoked creations.

Pickling

Almost everyone has had pickled fish; it's a delicious preservation method that has gained widespread acceptance. Pickling consists of two steps. First, the fish is brined with a dry or liquid brine. This removes excess water from the fish, and helps kill any potentially harmful parasites. The second stage of pickling involves immersing the brined fish in a flavored acidic solution for 1 to 4 days. There is some controversy over the relative safety of pickled fresh fish, and I have come to believe that fish should be frozen first to ensure complete safety when pickling. Depending on the size of the fish and the temperature of the freezer, from 2 to 7 days is ideal.

Most fish can be successfully pickled at home, but pickled halibut is a rare treat and one of my favorites. The simple, quick recipe for pickling halibut (page 111) would also work well for most any other type of fish.

Salting

The other preserving method that remains popular for at-home use is salting. This process helps remove water from the fish, firming the flesh and retarding spoilage. The most commonly seen salted fish dish is Gravlax, a Scandinavian salt- and sugar-cured salmon dish which is as easy as it is delicious.

On the following pages are some great ideas for curing, smoking and pickling as well as some dishes that use preserved fish.

BASIC HOT-SMOKED SALMON

Serves 6 to 8
Preparation: Overnight brining, plus several hours drying and smoking

1¹⁄₂ quarts (1.4 l) water

¹⁄₂ cup (145 g) pickling or kosher salt

¹⁄₄ cup (55 g) brown sugar

2 bay leaves

6 black peppercorns

3 pounds (1.36 kg) skin-on salmon fillet, pin bones removed

Hardwood or fruitwood chips, or special smoking sawdust

In saucepan, combine water, salt, brown sugar, bay leaves and peppercorns. Warm over low heat, stirring constantly, until salt and sugar are dissolved. Cool the brine. Place salmon fillet in glass or ceramic dish. Pour cooled brine over salmon; cover and refrigerate for 12 to 24 hours, turning once or twice.

Remove salmon fillet from brine, rinse with cool water and pat dry; discard brine. Allow salmon to air dry at room temperature, flesh side up, for 30 to 60 minutes, until a shiny, slightly sticky skin forms on the flesh (this is called a pellicle, and it helps prevent unsightly weeping when the fish is smoked).* Meanwhile, soak hardwood chips in a bucket of water, or spray smoking sawdust with water to dampen.

Smoke fish as directed in the instructions from your smoker, or follow the kettle-grill instructions on page 108 (also check the recipe for smoked sturgeon on page 112 for directions). Fish is done when it reaches an internal temperature of 160°F (70°C), usually from 1 to 3 hours. Serve hot, warm or cold.

*Many cooks direct a small fan over the fish, to speed formation of the pellicle. If it is particularly hot and humid in your kitchen and you don't use a fan, refrigerate the fish, uncovered, until the pellicle forms.

PICKLED HALIBUT & GRAVLAX

PICKLED HALIBUT

Serves 6 to 8
Preparation: 1 day brining, plus 1 or 2 days pickling

The longer the halibut remains in the pickling solution, the stronger the pickling flavor will become. Stored in the refrigerator, pickled fish should remain fresh-tasting for up to 2 weeks.

2 pounds (900 g) frozen boneless, skinless halibut fillets, thawed in refrigerator and cut into 1/2-inch (1.25 cm) cubes

3 tablespoons (54 g) pickling or kosher salt

PICKLING SOLUTION:

1 1/2 cups (3.5 dl) apple cider vinegar

1/2 cup (1.2 dl) distilled or filtered water

1/4 cup (55 g) brown sugar

1 tablespoon (5 g) pickling-spice blend

2 bay leaves

2 tablespoons (6.5 g) snipped fresh dill weed

6 black peppercorns

2 garlic cloves, peeled

1 large onion, thinly sliced

In medium glass or ceramic bowl, toss halibut chunks gently with salt. Cover and refrigerate for 24 hours.

After 24 hours, prepare the pickling solution: In medium stainless-steel saucepan, combine all pickling-solution ingredients. Heat just to boiling over high heat; remove from heat and set aside until completely cool. Rinse fish carefully with cold water; drain well and put in clean glass or ceramic bowl. Scatter onion slices over fish. Pour cooled pickling solution over fish and onions. Cover bowl with plastic wrap and refrigerate for 24 to 48 hours, gently stirring once or twice a day. Drain and serve.

CEVICHE

Serves 6 to 8
Preparation: 7 to 8 hours marinating

In this classic South American dish, raw fish is "cooked" with citrus juice.

1 pound (454 g) frozen boneless, skinless halibut, snapper, seabass or rockfish fillets, thawed in refrigerator and thinly sliced

1/4 cup (60 ml) freshly squeezed lime juice

1/4 cup (60 ml) freshly squeezed lemon juice

1 red onion, diced

1/2 cup (90 g) diced fresh tomatoes

1/4 cup (37 g) diced red bell pepper

1/4 cup (37 g) diced green bell pepper

1/4 cup (10 g) chopped cilantro

1/2 teaspoon (3 g) salt

1/4 teaspoon (.5 g) pepper

In medium glass or ceramic bowl, combine halibut, lime juice and lemon juice; stir gently to combine. Cover with plastic wrap and refrigerate for 6 hours. Pour off and discard marinade. Add remaining ingredients; stir gently to combine. Re-cover and refrigerate for 1 to 2 hours longer.

GRAVLAX

Serves 8 to 12
Preparation: 3 to 4 days marinating

Before you start, clear enough shelf space in the refrigerator to hold the dish with the salmon.

1/4 cup (72 g) salt, preferably kosher

3 tablespoons (37 g) sugar

1 tablespoon (6 g) coarsely ground black pepper

2 frozen skin-on salmon fillets (about 1 pound/ 454 g each), thawed in refrigerator, pin bones removed

1 cup (40 g) snipped fresh dill weed

1/4 cup (60 ml) vodka (flavored or plain) or brandy

In small bowl, mix together salt, sugar and pepper; sprinkle salt mixture evenly over flesh side of both salmon fillets. Place 1 fillet, skin-side down, in glass or ceramic baking dish; cover evenly with dill. Drizzle vodka over both pieces of salmon and place second fillet, flesh-side down, on top of fillet in dish. Cover dish with plastic wrap. Place in refrigerator; put a smaller sheet pan on top, and place 2 to 3 pounds of weight (cans work well) on sheet pan. Leave in refrigerator for 72 to 96 hours, pouring off accumulated liquid once a day. Slice very thinly against the grain and at a slight angle, and serve as a beautiful and delicate appetizer or light lunch.

ROSEMARY- AND APPLEWOOD-SMOKED STURGEON

Serves 6 to 8
Preparation: About 3 hours

The prehistoric-looking sturgeon is absolutely one of my favorite fish. It was once very plentiful but became over-fished in the last 30 years or so. More recently, it has been carefully controlled and is now more available both as a commercial and sport-caught fish. Sturgeon has one of the richest and oiliest meats of any fish, and thus is a perfect match for grilling or smoking.

3 pounds (1.36 kg) skinless sturgeon fillet

1/2 cup (145 g) kosher salt

1/4 cup (55 g) sugar

3 tablespoons (5 g) chopped fresh rosemary

1 teaspoon (2 g) pepper

2 shallots, minced

Approximately 3 cups (350 g) applewood chips

3 tablespoons (45 ml) olive oil

Place sturgeon in glass baking dish. In small bowl, combine salt, sugar, rosemary, pepper and shallots. Cover both sides of sturgeon evenly with salt mixture. Cover dish and refrigerate for 1 to 2 hours.

About 15 minutes before you are ready to grill, soak applewood chips in water; start charcoal grill, using about 8 cups charcoal briquettes in kettle-type grill that has a tight-fitting cover. When coals are ashed, spread them out and put soaked wood chips on top of briquettes. Cover grill and close all air vents, allowing chips to smolder for 2 to 3 minutes. Meanwhile, rinse sturgeon carefully with cold water, pat dry, and rub oil on both sides. Put sturgeon, skinned side up, on grate over coals; cover with lid and open an air vent slightly. Smoke for 10 minutes. Turn sturgeon skinned side down; re-cover and continue smoking for 10 to 15 minutes longer, or until cooked through.

COLD-SMOKED SALMON PÂTÉ

Serves 6 to 8
Preparation: Under 15 minutes

Serve this easy spread on toast points or crackers.

8 ounces (225 g) cold-smoked salmon (lox), roughly chopped

8 ounces (225 g) cream cheese

2 tablespoons (30 g) mayonnaise

2 tablespoons (6.5 g) snipped fresh dill weed

1 tablespoon (15 g) Dijon mustard

1 tablespoon (15 ml) lemon juice

1/4 teaspoon (.5 g) white pepper

1 shallot, minced

1 teaspoon (5 ml) cream, approximate

Combine salmon, cream cheese, mayonnaise, dill, mustard, lemon juice, pepper and shallot in food processor fitted with metal blade. Process until smooth, adding cream as necessary if mixture is too thick to process.

ESCABECHE OF ROCKFISH OR SNAPPER

Serves 4 to 6
Preparation: About 3 hours

An escabeche is a form of pickling that is often used in Portugal and Spain. It is similar to Ceviche (page 111), but with an escabeche the fish is cooked before pickling.

1/4 cup (35 g) all-purpose flour

1 tablespoon (5 g) paprika

1 teaspoon (6 g) salt

1/2 teaspoon (1 g) pepper

1/2 cup (1.2 dl) olive oil, divided

2 pounds (900 g) boneless, skinless rockfish or red snapper fillets

1/4 cup (60 ml) white wine vinegar

2 tablespoons (30 ml) freshly squeezed lemon juice

1 bunch flat-leaf (Italian) parsley, chopped

1 red onion, diced

4 cloves garlic, minced

In small bowl, stir together flour, paprika, salt and pepper. In large skillet, heat 1/4 cup (60 ml) of the oil over medium heat. When oil is hot but not smoking, dredge rockfish in seasoned flour; add to skillet and cook for 4 minutes per side, until just cooked through. Transfer rockfish to clean baking dish and cool in refrigerator. While fish is cooling, combine vinegar, lemon juice, parsley, onion, garlic and remaining 1/4 cup (60 ml) oil in medium glass or ceramic bowl; whisk to combine. Pour marinade over cooled fish. Cover dish and refrigerate for 1 to 2 hours. Remove fish from marinade and serve.

COLD-SMOKED SALMON PÂTÉ

PORTUGUESE SALT COD CAKES

Serves 4 to 6
Preparation: 2 days soaking, plus about 1 hour final preparation

1 pound (454 g) salt cod*

3 cups (330 g) breadcrumbs

3/4 cup (1.7 dl) olive oil, divided

2 tablespoons (10 g) paprika

2 tablespoons (8 g) chopped flat-leaf (Italian) parsley

2 tablespoons (6 g) chopped cilantro

1 tablespoon (1 g) dried basil

3 cloves garlic, minced

Lemon or lime juice for serving, optional

Place cod in large bowl and cover generously with water. Refrigerate for 48 hours, changing water 2 or 3 times each day. After soaking, cod should feel soft and fresh.

Put cod in medium saucepan, cover with cold water and heat to boiling over medium heat. Reduce heat to simmer and cook for 7 minutes. Drain cod; place in small bowl and refrigerate until cool enough to handle.

Flake cooled cod carefully, discarding any bones or skin; put flaked cod in mixing bowl. Add breadcrumbs, 1/2 cup (1.2 dl) of the oil, the paprika, parsley, cilantro, basil and garlic; mix gently but thoroughly. Gently form into 6 to 8 cakes, approximately 1/2 inch (1.25 cm) thick. Heat remaining 1/4 cup (60 ml) oil in large, heavy skillet over medium heat. When oil is hot and almost smoking, add cakes; cook for 2 to 3 minutes per side, until well browned. Serve hot as is, or with a little lemon or lime juice on top.

*SALT COD IS DRIED, HEAVILY SALTED COD THAT IS USED IN MEDITERRANEAN COOKING. LOOK FOR IT AT ITALIAN OR SPANISH SPECIALTY STORES, IN LARGE SUPERMARKETS OR IN SEAFOOD SHOPS.

BRANDADE

Serves 6 to 8
Preparation: 2 days soaking, plus about 1 hour final preparation

Serve this classic French dish warm with crackers or toast points as a rich and delicious first course or light supper.

1 pound (454 g) salt cod*

2 quarts (1.9 l) water

1 pound (454 g) potatoes

4 cloves garlic, roughly chopped

1/2 teaspoon (1 g) white pepper

1/2 teaspoon (3 g) salt

1/2 cup (1.2 dl) olive oil

2 tablespoons (30 ml) lemon juice

1/2 cup (1.2 dl) warm cream

Place cod in large bowl and cover generously with water. Refrigerate for 48 hours, changing water 2 or 3 times each day. After soaking, cod should feel soft and fresh.

Put cod in medium saucepan with water and heat to boiling over medium heat. Reduce heat to simmer and cook for 7 minutes. Drain cod; place in small bowl and refrigerate until cool enough to handle. Meanwhile, peel potatoes and add to saucepan with cod-cooking liquid. Boil over medium heat until tender. Drain potatoes, and mash or rice.

Flake cooled cod carefully, discarding any bones or skin. In food processor fitted with metal blade, combine flaked cod, mashed potatoes, garlic, pepper and salt. Turn processor on, and, with motor running, add olive oil and lemon juice. Finally, add cream through feed tube and process until smooth.

SMOKED SALMON AND POTATO SALAD

Serves 4 to 6
Preparation: 30 to 60 minutes

2 pounds (900 g) potatoes, cooked, peeled and cut into 3/4-inch (1.9 cm) pieces

1 pound (454 g) hot-smoked salmon, flaked

1/4 cup (60 ml) olive oil

2 tablespoons (3 g) minced fresh rosemary

1 tablespoon (15 ml) white wine vinegar

1 tablespoon (15 ml) balsamic vinegar

1/2 teaspoon (3 g) salt

1/4 teaspoon (.5 g) pepper

2 shallots, minced

In medium bowl, combine potatoes and salmon; stir gently. In separate bowl, whisk together oil, rosemary, wine vinegar, balsamic vinegar, salt, pepper and shallots. Pour dressing over salmon and potatoes; stir gently to combine. Cover and refrigerate for at least 30 minutes.

SOUR CREAM PICKLED SALMON

Serves 6 to 8
Preparation: 2 days marinating

PICKLING MIXTURE:

2 red onions, diced

2 cups (4.6 dl) white wine vinegar

1/2 cup (1.2 dl) distilled water

1/2 cup (110 g) brown sugar

1/4 cup (72 g) kosher or canning salt

2 tablespoons (6.5 g) snipped fresh dill weed

1 tablespoon (5 g) pickling-spice blend

2 pounds (900 g) frozen salmon fillet, thawed in refrigerator, pin bones removed

1 cup (227 g/2.3 dl) sour cream

2 teaspoons (6.5 g) drained capers

In medium stainless-steel saucepan, combine pickling-mixture ingredients; heat to boiling over high heat. Remove from heat; cool a bit, then refrigerate until cold.

Meanwhile, remove and discard skin and bones from salmon; cut salmon into 1/2-inch (1.25 cm) cubes and place in glass baking dish. Pour cooled pickling solution over salmon; cover with plastic wrap. Refrigerate for 48 hours, stirring gently several times each day. After 2 days, drain off and discard liquid. Gently fold sour cream and capers into pickled fish. Cover and refrigerate for at least 1 hour before serving.

SPICY CURED BLUEFISH OR MACKEREL "GRAVLAX"

Serves 8 to 12
Preparation: 2 to 3 days marinating

3 tablespoons (54 g) salt, preferably kosher

2 tablespoons (25 g) sugar

1 tablespoon (6 g) black pepper

1/4 teaspoon (.5 g) cayenne pepper

2 frozen skin-on bluefish or mackerel fillets (about 1 pound/454 g each), thawed in refrigerator, pin bones removed

1/2 cup (20 g) chopped cilantro

2 tablespoons (30 ml) lime juice

2 tablespoons (30 ml) tequila

In small bowl, mix together salt, sugar, black pepper and cayenne; sprinkle salt mixture evenly over flesh side of both fillets. Place 1 fillet, skin side down, in glass or ceramic baking dish; cover evenly with cilantro. Drizzle lime juice and tequila over the flesh side of both fillets and place second fillet, flesh side down, on top of fillet in dish. Cover dish with plastic wrap. Place in refrigerator; put a smaller sheet pan on top, and place 1 to 2 pounds (450 to 900 g) of weight (cans work well) on sheet pan. Leave in refrigerator for 48 to 72 hours, pouring off accumulated liquid once a day. To serve, slice very thinly against the grain and at a slight angle.

Nutrition Information

If a recipe has a range of servings, the data below applies to the greater number of servings. If the recipe lists a quantity range for an ingredient, the average quantity was used to calculate the nutritional data. If alternate ingredients are listed, the analysis applies to the first ingredient. If an ingredient cannot be accurately determined, NA is indicated.

	Calories	Fat (g)	Sodium (mg)	Saturated Fat (g)	Protein (g)	Carbohydrate (g)	Cholesterol (mg)
Apple, Blue Cheese & Pecan Salad	531	46	836	13	14	18	43
Asian Steamed Whole Flounder	284	12	893	2	28	12	67
Baked Bluefish w/Orange	260	13	93	2	31	2	90
Baked Grouper w/Garlic	330	12	133	2	36	14	63
Baked Halibut w/Saffron Sauce	532	38	178	18	37	4	152
Baked Lingcod w/Sauce	365	23	484	3	28	9	79
Balsamic Caesar Salad	183	16	149	3	5	5	31
Basic Boiled Shrimp	97	2	136	1	19	1	140
Basic Hot-Smoked Salmon	224	10	NA	2	30	2	84
Basic Pan-Fried Fish	417	17	123	2	36	27	131
Beurre Blanc	93	10	16	6	1	1	29
Billi-Bi Stew	481	46	633	28	10	6	172
Blackened Tuna	237	11	441	2	32	1	51
Bouillabaisse	463	29	452	4	31	19	57
Branade	372	20	NA	6	37	9	107
Cajun Barbecued Shrimp	232	18	178	5	14	4	114
Cajun Pan-Fried Oysters	381	22	397	2	11	34	80
Caribbean Okra & Shrimp	210	7	178	1	25	12	173
Ceviche	79	1	179	1	12	4	18
Chesapeake Bay Crab Cakes	246	13	685	5	19	13	129
Chinese Black Bean BBQ Sauce	40	2	328	1	1	5	0
Coconut Curried Salmon	561	36	123	8	36	25	89
Cold Octopus Salad	253	15	149	2	22	7	68
Cold Oven-Poached Salmon	467	40	335	9	23	4	92
Cold Smoked Salmon Pâté	162	14	716	7	7	1	41
Crab Dip	308	25	408	13	16	5	122
Crab Dumplings	267	6	495	1	17	35	62
Crab-Stuffed Mushroom Caps	265	21	476	4	16	6	65
Crab-Stuffed Mushrooms	188	13	234	3	13	7	43
Crabmeat Casserole	297	16	637	9	24	13	113
Crispy Mustard-Baked Mackerel	465	33	277	7	33	5	121
Crispy Parmesan Fish Fillets	232	10	267	4	28	7	76

	Calories	Fat (g)	Sodium (mg)	Saturated Fat (g)	Protein (g)	Carbohydrate (g)	Cholesterol (mg)
Cuban Fish w/Almond Sauce	409	21	124	2	34	21	42
Cucumber & Mustard Sauce	46	5	83	1	1	1	5
Curried Stuffed Lobster	531	35	709	4	30	23	91
Escabeche of Rockfish	294	16	482	2	29	7	53
Fish Fillets Baked in Parchment	241	10	151	4	36	1	70
Fish Fillets Baked w/Butter	299	13	197	6	42	1	87
Fish Steak Misoyaki	369	14	1,323	3	45	13	67
Fish Steaks Stuffed w/Feta	397	23	792	11	43	3	119
Fish Stock	10	1	264	0	1	2	0
Fried Halibut Cheeks w/Sauce	259	16	464	1	20	9	29
Fried Plantains	248	14	199	1	1	33	0
Fried Shad Roe w/Bacon	197	12	384	4	15	9	189
Garlic Mashed Potatoes	237	12	369	7	4	29	37
Gin & Peppercorn Sauce	40	3	20	2	1	1	8
Gravlax	67	4	NA	1	7	1	20
Greek Shrimp w/Feta & Olives	383	22	844	8	30	12	206
Grilled Herb-Stuffed Salmon	254	13	120	2	30	1	81
Grilled Marinated Fish Steaks	335	23	148	4	30	1	59
Grilled Swordfish w/Sauce	200	9	462	2	21	8	40
Harissa	78	7	78	1	1	4	0
Hawaiian Sesame Seed Sauce	99	9	516	1	1	4	0
Hazelnut Striped Bass	390	22	139	3	38	9	159
Hush Puppies	219	11	512	1	4	25	38
Indian Dry Curried Shrimp	203	9	461	2	24	6	173
Italian Sautéed Seabass	303	16	829	2	29	9	62
Lobster Risotto	367	11	659	3	17	50	30
Louisiana Shrimp Sauce	239	15	384	2	19	6	140
Malaysian Shrimp Fritters	193	6	224	1	15	19	139
Manhattan-Style Clam Chowder	181	10	205	1	7	18	12
Marlin Fajitas	497	18	494	3	34	48	53
Mexican Redfish w/Cilantro	409	30	696	4	29	4	64
Mussels & Fettuccine	397	10	521	5	15	61	33

	Calories	Fat (g)	Sodium (mg)	Saturated Fat (g)	Protein (g)	Carbohydrate (g)	Cholesterol (mg)
New England Clam Chowder	303	22	297	12	7	14	67
Oysters Rockefeller	224	15	355	4	12	10	42
Oyster Stew	637	61	625	37	13	11	272
Paella	282	8	365	1	20	33	108
Pasta Puttanesca	499	15	1,172	2	20	70	20
Pasta w/Rosemary & Fish	557	23	1,201	13	20	62	79
Peach, Onion & Pepper Salsa	410	28	9	4	4	43	0
Peppered Tuna Steak	304	12	72	3	42	4	67
Pickled Halibut	130	3	NA	1	24	1	36
Pineapple Salsa	48	1	2	1	1	10	0
Poached Steelhead w/Sauce	388	26	216	9	31	6	117
Poke	116	6	152	1	13	1	22
Polenta	229	4	338	1	6	41	2
Pompano in Parchment	576	38	266	11	49	7	127
Portuguese Salt Cod Cakes	683	32	NA	5	55	41	115
Portuguese Steamed Clams	283	19	487	6	13	8	41
Remoulade Sauce	74	8	77	1	1	1	6
Roast Asparagus	111	10	585	1	3	4	0
Roast Asparagus w/Salmon	181	15	818	2	9	3	9
Roasted New Potatoes	200	9	399	1	3	27	0
Rock Shrimp w/Cashews	331	22	231	7	26	7	188
Rosemary & Applewood Sturgeon	197	8	NA	2	27	2	102
Rouille	2,250	239	1,592	33	14	31	638
Saffron Rice	202	5	409	1	5	38	0
Salad Niçoise	620	48	308	8	31	18	179
Salmon & Shrimp Mousse	271	23	543	12	14	2	178
Salmon Baked w/Mushrooms	416	26	216	5	35	8	100
Salmon Steamed in Napa Cabbage	363	27	211	12	24	4	121
Salmon-Phyllo Wraps	323	22	333	9	14	17	65
Sautéed Scallops w/Mustard	272	15	311	5	21	11	65
Sautéed Soft-Shell Crab	269	16	1,295	5	19	13	173
Sautéed Sole w/Pecan Butter	414	27	226	7	34	10	105
Sautéed Sturgeon w/Wine	267	15	474	3	26	6	91
Sautéed Weakfish w/Bacon	371	23	601	6	27	13	126
Scallop & Corn Chowder	423	27	806	13	18	22	92
Seafood Gumbo	269	14	654	1	24	12	142
Seafood-Stuffed Grape Leaves	289	17	1,801	3	18	2	29

	Calories	Fat (g)	Sodium (mg)	Saturated Fat (g)	Protein (g)	Carbohydrate (g)	Cholesterol (mg)
Seared Shark w/Tomato Salsa	331	18	143	3	37	4	87
Seared Tuna w/Pesto	680	51	547	10	51	6	75
Seared Yellowtail & Salad	252	20	284	4	16	2	36
Shermoula	269	9	81	2	23	24	47
Shrimp Creole	312	12	257	2	32	12	230
Shrimp, Mango & Potato Curry	291	11	472	4	26	23	189
Shrimp, Mushroom & Herb Omelet	619	41	599	19	46	18	872
Simple Steamed Mussels	42	1	170	1	5	2	12
Simple Tuna Chowder	555	32	904	5	28	29	38
Skate w/Black Butter & Capers	387	24	594	14	37	2	156
Skewered Teriyaki Shrimp	129	6	1,011	1	14	5	93
Smoked Salmon & Potato Salad	352	16	1,260	2	23	30	56
Smoked Salmon Cakes	275	16	986	4	15	19	109
Sole Florentine	469	27	299	8	49	9	124
Sour Cream Pickled Salmon	217	12	459	5	21	4	69
Southern Garlic Greens	118	8	197	3	4	8	10
Spanish Almond Fennel Sauce	35	3	19	1	1	2	0
Spiced Fish w/Tamarind & Coconut	357	19	112	8	33	12	56
Spicy Cured Bluefish	91	3	NA	1	14	1	40
Spicy Squid Flowers	186	11	394	2	13	9	176
Squid w/Rich Red Wine Sauce	159	11	60	3	10	7	140
Steamed Clams w/Ginger	60	4	141	2	3	3	18
Steamed Mussels & Grand Marnier	364	29	275	18	9	11	115
Steamed Striper w/Scallops	201	4	199	1	36	4	136
Stir-Fried Scallops w/Champagne	215	13	224	5	13	8	46
Striped Bass Baked w/Fennel	276	12	509	2	26	9	109
Szechuan Braised Fish	240	11	440	2	26	8	44
Tandoori-Style Yogurt Marinade	10	1	34	1	1	1	1
Tapenade	48	4	279	1	1	2	2
Tartar Sauce	67	7	122	1	1	1	5
Teriyaki Sauce	16	0	172	0	1	3	0
Thai Shrimp Soup	171	6	601	4	21	8	144
Tuna Carpaccio w/Mayonnaise	463	41	76	6	19	3	100
Warm Green Bean & Hazelnut Salad	212	19	47	3	5	8	71
Whole Fish Baked w/Mustard	265	11	166	2	28	3	51
Wild Rice Pilaf	204	10	412	2	6	24	5

Glossary of Cooking Methods

Here are a few tips to help you prepare each recipe for its fullest flavor. Have fun trying some new options.

Steaming, Poaching and Boiling

These methods all involve cooking with water or a flavorful liquid such as wine, champagne, stock, court bouillon, fruit juice or apple cider. Herbs, spices, garlic, shallots or vegetables may be added to flavor the liquid as desired.

In steaming, the food is generally placed on a rack that lifts it above the liquid; however, shellfish is often steamed by placing it directly in the bottom of the pan with a half-inch or so of liquid. In either case, the pan is covered tightly, creating the steam that cooks the seafood. You may steam in virtually any size pan or pot large enough to hold the seafood in a single layer.

In poaching, seafood is added to a pan containing enough simmering liquid to completely cover it. The seafood is simmered, uncovered, until just cooked through. Boiling is similar to poaching, except that higher heat is used to keep the liquid at a continuous boil.

Fin fish: Poached salmon is a classic dish, but many other fish take well to poaching. Try seasoning the liquid with thyme, rosemary, marjoram or other mild herbs. Extremely firm fish such as tuna or extremely flaky fillets like sole or cod do not work as well as salmon, steelhead and skate. Many fish species are used in soups or stews, but simple boiling is not recommended for fish.

Shellfish: Steaming is probably the most common preparation for oysters, mussels, clams and live scallops in the shell. These shellfish should all be steamed just until their shells open. Remove the shellfish from the steamer as soon as the shells open, although an extra minute or two won't hurt them. If some haven't opened a few minutes after the rest have, discard them; any bivalves that don't open during steaming were dead before they went into the pan, and are not edible.

Lobsters steam beautifully and quickly, and many people consider this the most flavorful way to cook lobster. Put the lobster on a rack over the boiling liquid and cover tightly; a 1¼ pound (570 g) lobster should steam for approximately 10 minutes. For larger lobsters add about 5 minutes for each additional pound (454 g) and remember not to overcrowd your pot.

Shrimp may be thrown into the boiling steaming liquid with shells on or off; a rack is not necessary, but you may use one if you like. Shrimp take 2 to 5 minutes to steam, depending on their size. To determine doneness, look for red shells and meat that is opaque all the way through.

Boiling is a popular alternative for shrimp, lobsters or crabs. Cooking times should be very similar to steaming times, perhaps slightly less. Feel free to add seasoning to your boiling liquid. Bay leaves, peppercorns and onions are common additions when boiling shellfish.

Sautéing and Pan-Frying

Sautéing and pan-frying are related cooking methods, in which foods are cooked with oil in a hot skillet or sauté pan over moderate to high heat. The primary difference is the amount of oil used; for pan-frying, the bottom of the skillet should be coated with about ¼ inch (.6 cm) of oil, while much less is used for sautéing. A heavy pan is best; cast iron, sandwiched aluminum or layered stainless steel all work well. Canola, safflower or sunflower oils work particularly well as they all have a high smoking point and are neutrally flavored. You may also use more assertive oils such as olive oil or dark (Asian) sesame oil; butter adds a great flavor to a sauté, but will burn if the heat is too high.

Seafood to be pan-fried is generally given a light breading before cooking, while just a dusting of flour—or more frequently, no coating at all—may be called for when sautéing.

Always make sure the oil is hot before you add the seafood; in pan-frying, the oil should be heated almost to the smoking point. If cut-up seafood, or smaller pieces of seafood such as scallops, is sautéed, it should be stirred frequently to ensure even cooking. After sautéing, you may add a little liquid, such as lemon juice, vinegar or wine, and perhaps some seasoning, to the pan for a quick and wonderful pan sauce (this does not work with pan-frying). Acidic sauces such as tartar, remoulade, Tabasco, lemon and caper go very well with pan-fried seafood.

Fin fish: Milder, less oily and flaky fish work best for sautéing and pan-frying; very firm or oily fish are not generally sautéed, due to the added oil. To sauté fish fillets, heat a small amount of oil or butter in a heavy skillet. Lightly dust fillets with flour, cornmeal or ground nuts. Place fillets, skin side down, in skillet and cook over medium-high heat until browned; turn and brown the second side. Cooking times are short, generally just a few minutes per side.

For pan-frying, coat the bottom of a heavy skillet with ¼ inch (.6 cm) of oil; heat until just below the smoking point. Dip the fish in an egg wash (egg beaten with 2 tablespoons/30 ml of milk or water). Roll the fish in a coating of flour, cornmeal or cracker crumbs. Fry over medium heat for 3 to 5 minutes per inch of thickness per side.

Shellfish: Shrimp and scallops are particularly suited to sautéing. Both cook very quickly, 2 to 5 minutes depending on size. Shrimp may be sautéed with shells on or off, depending on your preference and recipe.

Baking (Roasting)

Select a dish that holds the seafood comfortably—neither crowded nor so large that the seafood becomes "lost" in the dish. Seafood is generally baked in a hot oven (400°F to 450°F/205°C to 230°C) for a relatively short time. The Canadian Rule, which states that fish should be cooked for 8 to 10 minutes per inch (2.5 cm) of thickness, also works surprisingly well for shellfish. Make sure you estimate the total depth of all your ingredients and not just the shellfish for timing purposes.

Fin fish: Almost any fish can be baked. Place fish in a single layer, skin down, in an oiled or buttered dish (or add 1/8 inch/.3 cm of liquid to the dish). Season with butter or sauce if desired. If your fillet is of uneven thickness, fold the tail under so the thickness is relatively even.

Oily fish stand up to more acidic seasonings such as vinegar, strong citrus or pepper combinations. Leaner fish, because of their drier, milder-tasting flesh, go better with added oils or butter and less-assertive seasonings.

Shellfish: As with fin fish, almost any shellfish can be baked. In most cases all you need is a heavy baking pan, some liquid and whatever seasoning you choose. Mussels, for example, may be put in a pan with tomatoes, garlic and olive oil and baked until the shells open. Scallops bake wonderfully, topped perhaps with some mustard, bread crumbs, garlic, olive oil and white wine. If you wish to roast lobsters or crabs, lightly crack the shells, and keep moist with oil or butter and a little added liquid.

Broiling

Adjust your oven rack so it is about 4 inches from the heat source. Preheat at broil; if your oven has no broiling capacity, you may simulate broiling by baking, uncovered, in a 550°F (288°C) oven. Shellfish is seldom broiled, except perhaps for a few minutes after baking to provide a nice finish to a casserole dish.

Fin fish: Firm, oily or moderately oily fish work best. Most flaky fish work well when thicker cuts are used, but leaner fish have a tendency to dry out. Place fish steaks or fillets in a heavy pan or on a baking sheet. Baste both sides with oil or butter; this adds flavor and protects the fish from drying and is especially important with leaner, more flaky fish. Broil approximately 8 minutes per inch (2.5 cm) of thickness, allowing the first side to broil about 75 percent of the

total cooking time before turning the fish over to finish. For a nice touch, try using flavored oils, marinades or herb butters for basting.

Grilling (Barbecuing)

Grilling adds a wonderful taste that is simultaneously sweet, smoky and sharp, and works well for many types of seafood. Charcoal briquettes or natural-wood charcoal should be at the "ashed" stage, which takes 15 or 20 minutes after lighting; gas grills should be preheated for at least 5 minutes prior to cooking. For most seafood recipes, a covered grill is often the best choice. The cover helps prevent flare-ups from dripping oil or fat, and provides more even heat; it also concentrates the smoke for more flavor.

Fin fish: Firm fish with a moderate to high oil content are the best choices for grilling. As with baking, oily fish stand up to stronger seasonings, while leaner fish are better with less-assertive flavorings. Marinating adds flavor and helps protect fish from drying out, but should be done for a short time only, generally 30 to 45 minutes; longer times may cause the fish to become mushy. Brush the hot grate (and both sides of the fish, if not marinated) with oil to prevent sticking. Cooking time will be 8 to 10 minutes per inch (2.5 cm) of thickness; turn the fish just once during cooking. Basting with a marinade, butter or oil helps keep the fish moist and flavorful, particularly if cooking time is longer than a few minutes. Flaky fish require the use of a screen or piece of foil for support.

Shellfish: The natural brininess of shellfish and the sweet smoke of grilling is a combination that is out of this world. Larger shellfish such as oysters, lobsters or crabs can be thrown directly on the grate, while smaller shellfish like shrimp, scallops, mussels or clams should be skewered or put on a screen. Timing is essentially the same as for baking: 8 to 10 minutes per inch (2.5 cm) of thickness or, for mussels, clams or oysters, until their shells open.

As with baking, the trick is to keep the shellfish moist while grilling; basting with a flavored oil or butter during cooking will help, and you need not bother turning. Lobsters can be split and grilled with a curry-and-chutney butter with amazing results. A skewer of shrimp and vegetables with a Cajun marinade makes a perfect 5-minute meal.

A Final Note About Fin Fish

Here's a tip to help you get great-looking and great-tasting fish. Fish fillets have a "round" and a "flat" side. The flat side is the skin side, which usually has connective tissue that reacts to heat by contracting, causing the fillet to curl. Therefore, when cooking fish fillets, always start with the skin side away from the heat source. For instance, when grilling, sautéing or pan-frying, start with the skin side up. When baking, where the heat tends to rise, start with the skin side down. This will not only eliminate most curling but also will help ensure even, consistent cooking times.

Substitutions

One of the challenges in learning to cook fish is the vast variety of species available. In my cooking classes, I have seen students struggle as their purchase or catch doesn't match their selected recipe. What do you do when you have just caught a beautiful seatrout but you can't find any appealing seatrout recipes? Perhaps you have picked out a recipe for baked pompano but your fish store has no pompano that day. Luckily, it is a simple process to learn which fish makes a proper substitution for another fish.

To substitute one fish for another, look at these characteristics, given in order of importance: oil content, flavor strength and texture. For example, if I find a recipe for bluefish, but cannot catch or buy bluefish, I will look for fish with similar attributes: oily, strong flavored and soft textured. In contrast, a recipe for halibut requires a lean, mild and flaky alternative.

Whenever possible I base my seafood choice not on a particular recipe but rather on the quality and value of my available options. If my supermarket has pristine tuna on sale, I will find a suitable recipe for it rather than purchase an over-the-hill or overpriced swordfish steak. A sterling rockfish fillet will be infinitely more rewarding than a mediocre halibut fillet.

The substitutions below go both ways. If you have a recipe for a particular fish, use this guide to find an appropriate substitute for the fish listed in the recipe; on the other hand, if you have a particular type of fish, look for a recipe that features any of the listed substitutes. This is quite useful to the sport angler, who may find it easier to catch a particular fish than to find a recipe for it.

The listings below cover the most popular saltwater fin fish (although some are anadromous, migrating from fresh to saltwater and back). For a quick overview of possible fish substitutions, also see the chart on page 20.

Arctic char (Salvelinus alpinus)

A relative of the salmon; like salmon, char can be freshwater, saltwater or anadromous. Farm-raised and wild-caught. A moderately oily fish with medium-strength flavor and flaky flesh. May be grilled, baked, poached or sautéed. Substitutes: Salmon, trout, steelhead.

Atlantic cod (Gadus morhua)

An extremely popular lean, flaky white fish with a very mild flavor. May be baked, sautéed, fried or steamed. Substitutes: Haddock, rockfish, lingcod.

Atlantic salmon (Salmo salar)

Commercially, this is exclusively a farm-raised fish, although many people enjoy fly fishing for these beautiful salmon. The orange to red flesh of this salmon is oily and flaky and yet has a relatively mild flavor. May be baked, grilled, poached, steamed, braised, broiled or sautéed. Substitutes: Any other salmon or steelhead.

Barracuda (Sphyraena argentea)

Must be caught in areas away from coral reefs to protect against ciguatera, a potentially dangerous toxin sometimes picked up by reef-feeding fish. Barracuda has delicious grayish blue flesh with a high oil content, firm meat and a medium flavor strength similar to pork tenderloin. May be grilled, baked or sautéed. Substitutes: Marlin, sea trout, cobia.

Black cod (Anoplopoma fimbria)

Also known as sablefish or butterfish. Highly prized, extremely oily fish with ivory-colored flesh, buttery sweet and mild flavor, flaky texture. May be baked, grilled, seared, steamed, sautéed or smoked. Substitutes: Tuna, sturgeon, lingcod.

Bluefish (Pomatomus saltatrix)

A great sport fish that is also fished commercially. Blueish gray flesh, high oil content, strong flavor and soft texture. May be baked, grilled, smoked or broiled. Substitutes: Mackerel, sea trout, redfish, pompano.

Bonito

Atlantic bonito (Sarda sarda), Pacific bonito (Sarda chiliensis)

A small tuna-like fish, usually from 2 to 6 pounds (1 to 3 kg). Flesh is oily and firm, with a medium to strong flavor profile. Bonito may be baked, broiled, grilled or smoked. Substitutes: Tuna, mackerel, marlin, cobia.

Chilean Seabass (Dissostichus eleginoides)

Also known as Patagonian toothfish. Not a seabass at all, although it has become known as one. It has jumped in popularity over the last few years and what once was a very inexpensive fish has now become much more expensive. This increased popularity has led to allegations of overfishing. A very mild fish with firm, flaky texture and high oil content. May be baked, grilled, seared, steamed, poached, sautéed or broiled. Substitutes: Black cod, sturgeon, swordfish.

Chinook salmon, see: King salmon

Cobia *(Rachycentron canadum)*

Also known as lemon fish. Caught in the Atlantic and Gulf. Firm, sweet flesh with medium oil content and mild to medium flavor strength. May be baked, broiled, grilled or sautéed. Substitutes: Swordfish, marlin, shark.

Cod, see: Black cod

Coho salmon *(Oncorhynchus kisutch)*

Also known as silver salmon, these are primarily a wild-caught species although a few are still farm-raised in New Zealand and Canada. Coho is a slightly milder salmon than the sockeye or king salmon, but nonetheless has oily flesh, medium firm flake and a moderately strong salmon flavor. May be baked, grilled, poached, steamed, braised, broiled, smoked or sautéed. Substitutes: Steelhead or any other salmon.

Corbina *(Menticirrhus undulatus)*

Also known as a white seabass, this relative of the croaker and drum families is a sought-after species both for sport anglers and commercial operations alike. Moderately flaky, with medium oil content and a rich, sweet taste. May be sautéed, baked, broiled, steamed or smoked. Substitutes: Seatrout, redfish, snook, snapper.

Flounder *(Limanda ferruginea, Atlantic flounder)*

Also known as dab. One of many related flatfish such as fluke and lemon sole. Collectively, these fish are commonly referred to as sole, although the only true sole is the Dover sole from Europe. All of these fish have very mild, soft and flaky flesh and very low oil content. May be steamed, baked, sautéed or fried. Substitutes: Cod, any other flounder, halibut.

Grouper *(Epinephelus morio, red grouper)*

A family of fish that includes the most commonly seen red grouper. All have mild, sweet and relatively firm but still flaky flesh with low oil content. May be baked, broiled, sautéed, steamed, fried or grilled. Substitutes: Snapper, seabass, any other grouper.

Haddock *(Melanogrammus aeglefinus)*

These "high-end" members of the cod family have lean, mild-tasting flesh and a flaky texture. May be baked, broiled, steamed, poached, fried or sautéed. Substitutes: Halibut, cod, rockfish, sole.

Halibut

Atlantic halibut *(Hippoglossus hippoglossus)*,
Pacific halibut *(Hippoglossus stenolepis)*

A large flatfish and relative of the flounder family with sweet, flaky white flesh with low oil content. Pacific halibut is primarily caught from Alaska to Northern California. May be baked, fried, sautéed, steamed, poached or carefully grilled. Substitutes: Grouper, cod, haddock, rockfish, seabass, snapper, tautog.

John Dory *(Zeus faber)*

A famous and world-renowned fish that comes from areas as diverse as New Zealand, the Mediterranean, the British Isles and the Northeast coast of the United States. These fish have a distinguishing thumbprint on their sides, supposedly the mark of St. Peter. Sweet, delicately flavored flesh with flaky texture and low oil content. May be baked, broiled, sautéed, steamed, fried or poached. Substitutes: Sole, flounder, halibut, seabass.

King salmon *(Oncorhynchus tshawytscha)*

Also known as a chinook, this is the largest member of the salmon family and, along with the sockeye, has the deepest flavor and highest oil content. Kings may be farm-raised although it is usually a wild-caught species. Rich, oily flesh with a firm flakiness and a pronounced flavor. May be baked, grilled, poached, steamed, braised, broiled, smoked or sautéed. Substitutes: Steelhead or any other salmon.

Lingcod *(Ophidon elongatus)*

A greenling rather than a cod. Highly renowned, especially on the West Coast. Green to white flesh is quite mild but still sweet, with large flaky texture and low to moderately low oil content. May be baked, broiled, grilled, steamed or fried. Substitutes: Halibut, rockfish, snapper, grouper, seabass.

Mackerel, Spanish *(Scomberomorus maculatus)*

The Spanish mackerel is one of the more common mackerels from a family that includes Atlantic mackerel, cerro mackerel and king mackerel (among many others). All have gray to red flesh with strong, assertive flavor, firmly flaky texture and high oil content. May be smoked, grilled, baked, braised or broiled. Substitutes: Any other mackerel, bluefish, redfish, seatrout, pompano.

Marlin

Blue marlin *(Makaira nigricans)*, Striped marlin *(Tetrapturus audax)*

These billfish are commercially caught in Hawaii and South America; Hawaiian marlin have more fat and are infinitely better tasting than South American marlin. Marlin has moderate flavor strength, firm texture and moderate to moderately high oil content. May be baked, grilled, stir-fried, braised or smoked. Substitutes: Wahoo, cobia, swordfish, tuna.

Monkfish *(Lophius americanus)*

A strange-looking fish also known as goosefish or anglerfish. Caught primarily for their tail muscles, which have a delicious, sweet and mild flavor, very firm texture and low to moderate oil content. The Asian and sushi trades also use monkfish livers. May be stir-fried, sautéed, braised, grilled or poached. Substitutes: Monk is a unique fish and appropriate substitutes are difficult to come by. For certain recipes cobia, scallops or even lobster meat may suffice.

Orange roughy *(Hoplostethus atlanticus)*

Found mostly around New Zealand and Australia, this very mild, flaky, lean fish gained great popularity in the seventies and eighties as an extremely inexpensive alternative to sole, halibut and cod. Roughy became overfished and grew to be quite expensive until recently, when it is neither overfished nor particularly popular. May be baked, sautéed or fried. Substitutes: Cod, sole, halibut, flounder.

Pompano *(Trachinotus carolinus)*

A small member of the jack family that is an absolutely delicious and delicate treat. Rich, oily flesh with moderate firmness and relatively full flavor. May be baked, grilled, steamed or sautéed. Substitutes: Redfish, seatrout, amberjack, yellowtail jack.

Porgy *(Stenotomus chrysops)*

Very similar to Eastern sheepshead (*Archosargus probatocephalus*). A very common East Coast panfish with mild, flaky flesh and a low oil content. May be sautéed, fried, baked or braised. Substitutes: Snapper, rockfish, seatrout, redfish.

Redfish *(Sciaenops ocellata)*

Also known as red drum. Perhaps the best-tasting member of the drum family. Almost exclusively sport-caught, although it is sometimes farm-raised. This once-plentiful fish fell victim to a huge burst of popularity fueled by the blackened redfish craze (originating with Paul Prudhomme's recipe). It is now illegal to commercially fish for redfish. Nutty, mild flavor when young (stronger as the fish gets large), flaky texture and moderate to high oil content. May be baked, braised, grilled, sautéed, broiled or smoked. Substitutes: Seatrout, snapper, mackerel.

Red snapper, American *(Lutianus campechanus)*

The snapper family consists of about 30 different species including the mangrove, mutton, lane and yellowtail snapper. American red snappers are considered by some to be the best of the snappers, but in my opinion many of the other snappers are equally as desirable. Snapper meat is lean, moderately full flavored with a firm, large flake. May be baked, grilled, steamed, broiled, sautéed or poached. Substitutes: Grouper, seabass, seatrout.

Rockfish *(Sebastes ruberrimus, yelloweye rockfish)*

Yelloweye is perhaps the best-tasting member of the rockfish family. This relative of the perch family is sometimes erroneously referred to as a red snapper. Rockfish has a mild flavor, a large firm flake, and low oil content. May be baked, broiled, grilled, sautéed, fried or steamed. Substitutes: Snapper, grouper, seabass.

Salmon

See listings for individual species: Atlantic salmon, Coho salmon, King salmon, Sockeye salmon.

Sand bass *(Paralabrax maculatofasciatus)*

A smallish saltwater bass found from mid-California to the sea of Cortez, these great sportfish have a mild flavor, flaky flesh and low oil content. May be sautéed, baked, broiled or steamed. Substitutes: Rockfish, striped bass, grouper, porgy.

Seabass

This is an "umbrella" term used to encompass many species including grouper, domestic and European bass, striped bass, black bass and loup de mer. Chilean seabass is technically not a seabass at all; see separate listing. Substitutes: Any of the fish mentioned here will work in a recipe calling for seabass.

Seatrout, see: Spotted seatrout, Weakfish

Shad *(Alosa sapidissima)*

An anadromous species found both in the Atlantic and Pacific, shad spawn in rivers from March to July. Often caught just for the roe, shad is nonetheless a delicious albeit bony fish with a high fat content, soft texture and strong flavor. May be baked, broiled, grilled or smoked. Substitutes: Mackerel, bluefish, seatrout. The roe has no substitute.

Shark

Mako (*Isurus glaucus*), Thresher (*Alopius vulpinus*)

Two of the best tasting and most popular sharks. Firm, moderately flavored flesh with a medium to low fat content. May be baked, grilled, stir-fried, broiled or sautéed. Substitutes: Swordfish, cobia, marlin.

Sheepshead *(Archosargus probatocephalus)*

A member of the porgy family, with very similar characteristics. See porgy listing for cooking and substitution information.

Skate *(Raja binoculata)*

A ray caught in both the Pacific and Atlantic Oceans. This underappreciated fish has very sweet, mild and lean flesh with a stringy flakiness similar in texture to crabmeat. May be poached, broiled, sautéed or steamed. Substitutes: Scallops or crabmeat work in some recipes.

Snook (Centropomus undecimalis)

This great-tasting fish is exclusively sport-caught. Low to medium oil content, moderately soft flesh, mild flavor. May be baked, broiled, sautéed or steamed. Substitutes: Striped bass, snapper, grouper.

Sockeye salmon (Oncorhynchus nerka)

Sockeye are a slightly smaller salmon (usually from 2 to 10 pounds/1 to 4.5 kg) with a very rich flavor, deep red oily flesh and a firm flake. Sockeyes are always wild-caught, and many people consider a good sockeye to be the pinnacle of fine eating. May be baked, grilled, poached, steamed, braised, broiled, sautéed or smoked. Substitutes: Steelhead or any other salmon.

Sole

This is a term used to describe any flatfish, including flounder, fluke and lemon sole (all of these are actually flounder). Technically, the only true sole is the Dover sole. Substitutes: Flounder, fluke, lemon sole, Dover sole.

Spotted seatrout (Cynoscion nebulosus)

Also called speckled trout. An extremely popular sportfish found primarily from Maryland south into the Gulf of Mexico. Weakfish is also called seatrout, but is a different species; see listing for weakfish. Spotted seatrout has flaky, soft flesh with a moderate to high oil content and a sweet, mild flavor. May be baked, braised, sautéed, broiled, smoked or grilled. Substitutes: Weakfish, yellowtail jack, redfish or red snapper.

Steelhead (Oncorhynchus mykiss)

An ocean-going rainbow trout, steelhead can grow to 25 pounds (10 kg). Delicious rich flesh with a medium flavor profile, high oil content and a medium flake like salmon. Baked, grilled, poached, steamed, braised, broiled or sautéed. Substitutes: Any salmon.

Striped bass (Morone saxatilis)

A popular marine gamefish that is also taken commercially, stripers may range from about 2 to 30 pounds (1 to 14 kg). A hybrid between freshwater striped bass and wild striped bass is also farm-raised (sometimes called "wipers"). Striped bass are flaky and lean to moderately lean with a sweet, mild flavor. Baked, broiled, grilled, sautéed, steamed or poached. Substitutes: Snapper, halibut, snook, grouper.

Sturgeon (Acipenser transmontanus, white sturgeon)

Found in both saltwater and fresh water, sturgeon was once very plentiful but fell victim to overfishing. The harvest has been carefully controlled, and sturgeon is now more readily available both as a commercial and sport-caught fish. Rich, firm, sweet meat with a high oil content. May be baked, grilled, steamed, broiled, sautéed or smoked. Substitutes: Marlin, cobia, swordfish, shark.

Swordfish (Xiphias gladius)

One of the largest members of the billfish family, swordfish have firm, whitish meat with a moderately mild, meaty flavor and a high fat content. May be baked, grilled, sautéed, steamed or smoked. Substitutes: Marlin, tuna, shark, wahoo.

Tautog (Tautoga onitis)

Also known as blackfish. This member of the wrasse family ranges from 1 to about 25 pounds (.4 to 10 kg). Because the primary item in their diet is shellfish, tautog have wonderfully sweet flesh with a low to medium oil content and a firm, flaky texture. Baked, broiled, grilled or sautéed. Substitutes: Striped bass, sheepshead, snapper.

Tripletail (Lobotes surinamensis)

This fish is called tripletail because the tail, anal and dorsal fins are close together and similarly sized. This delicious fish is regularly caught by sport anglers in the Atlantic, Pacific and Indian Oceans; it's also commercially fished. Moderately lean, flaky flesh with a sweet mild flavor. May be sautéed, baked, steamed or broiled. Substitutes: Striped bass, snapper, snook, grouper.

Tuna

Albacore tuna (Thunnus alalunga), Bluefin tuna (Thunnus thynnus), Yellowfin tuna (Thunnus albacaras)

Albacore is a smaller tuna with flesh that ranges from whitish gray to a deep, clear red; it has slightly less oil than other tuna but is still an oily, firm fish with a medium flavor strength. Bluefin tuna has the highest fat content of any tuna and is absolutely delicious; its firm meat is deep red. Yellowfin tuna has a deep red color, relatively strong, meaty flavor, very firm texture and a high oil content. All tuna may be baked, grilled, broiled, sautéed, stir-fried or smoked, and is also prized for sushi. Substitutes: Swordfish, marlin, shark, wahoo.

Weakfish (Cynoscion regalis)

Also known as seatrout, but not to be confused with spotted seatrout (see listing for spotted seatrout). An oily fish with a fine, nutty and sweet flesh and a delicate, flaky texture. May be baked, grilled, steamed or braised. Substitutes: Snapper, redfish or snook.

Yellowtail (Seriola dorsalis)

Also called hamachi or yellowtail jack. These are among the finest-tasting fish in the Pacific Ocean, and command a high price at the sushi market. Moderately strong flavor, high oil content and firm texture. May be baked, grilled, broiled, stir-fried, sautéed, smoked or eaten raw. Substitutes: Wahoo, marlin, cobia.

I N D E X